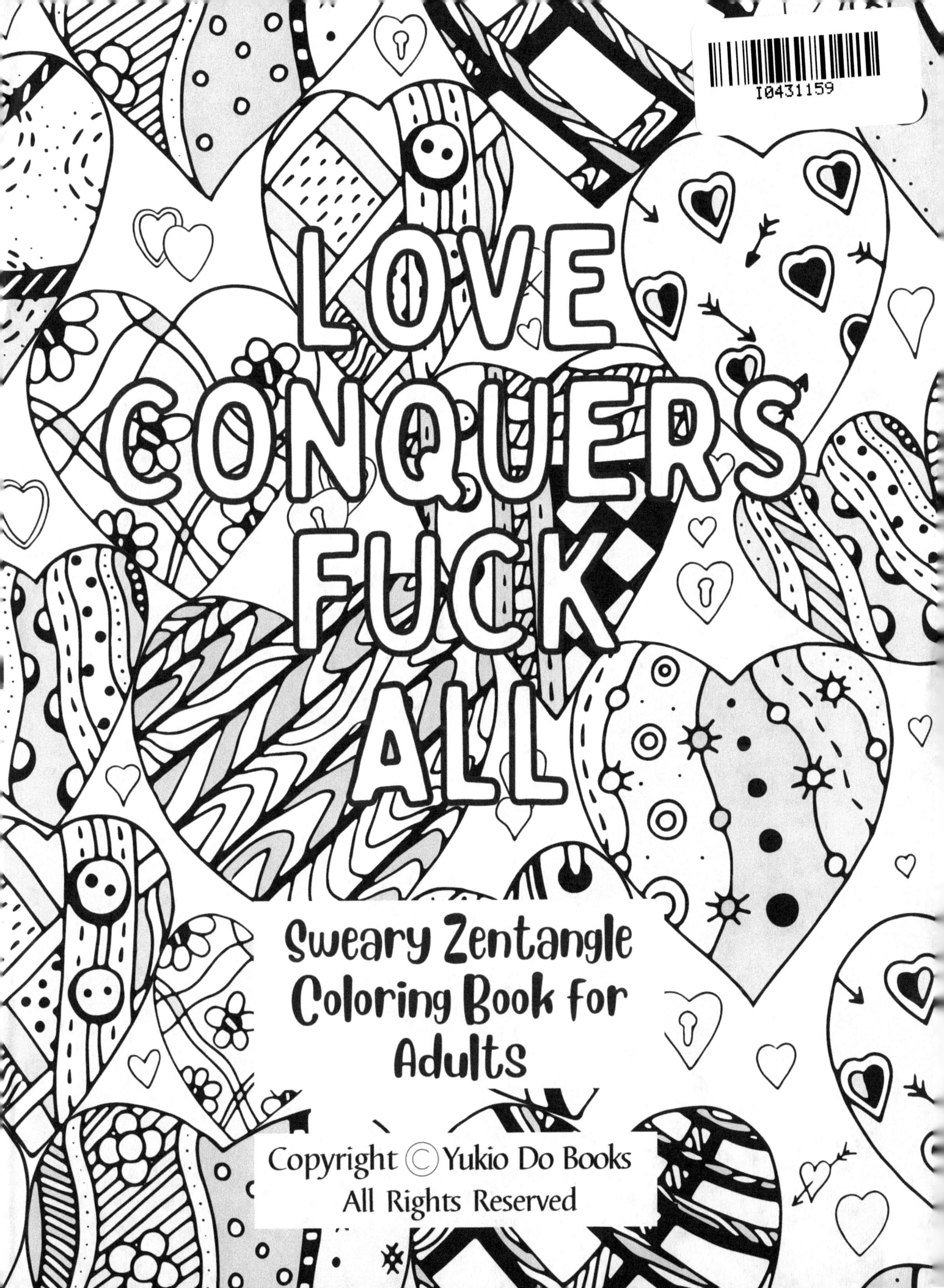

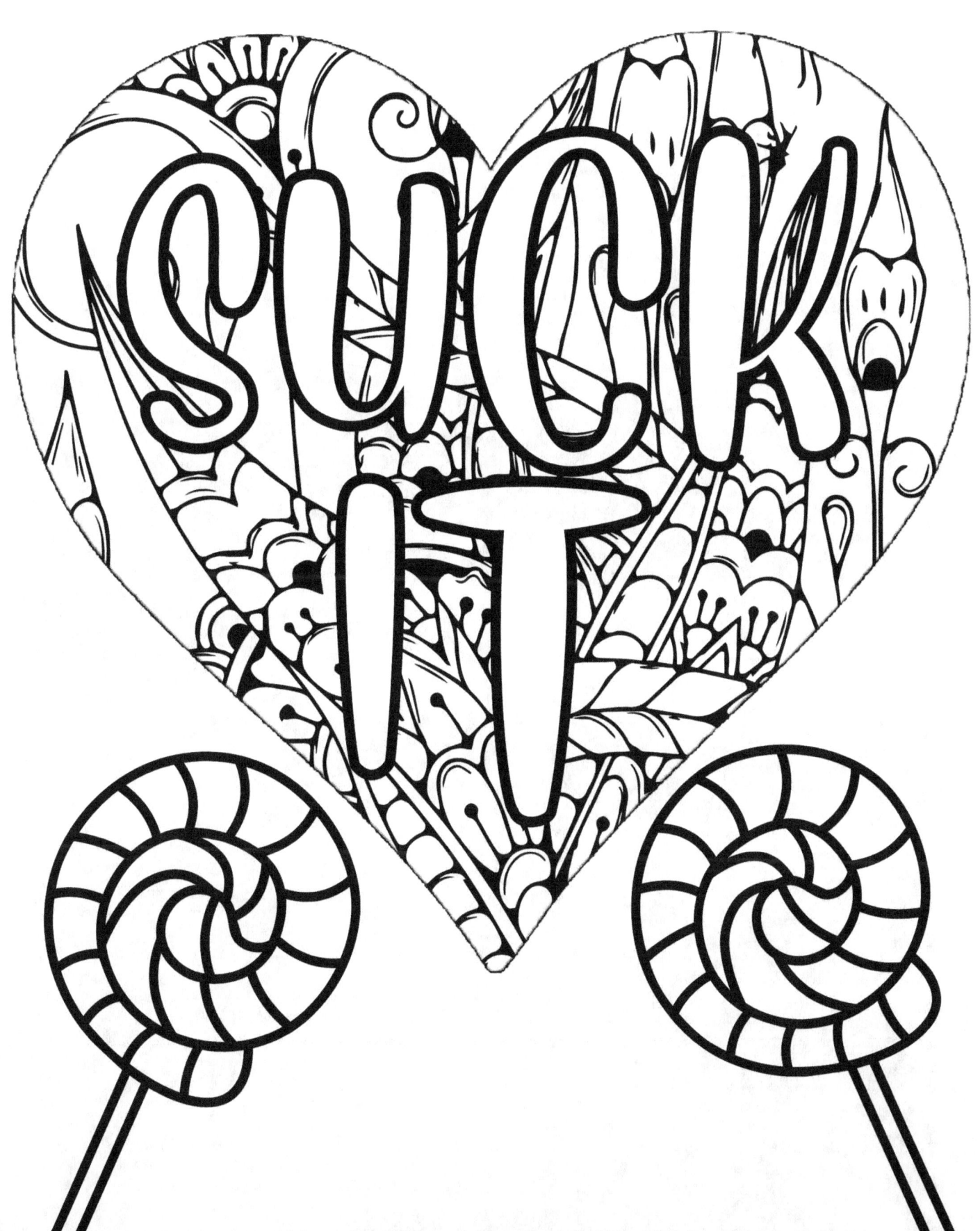

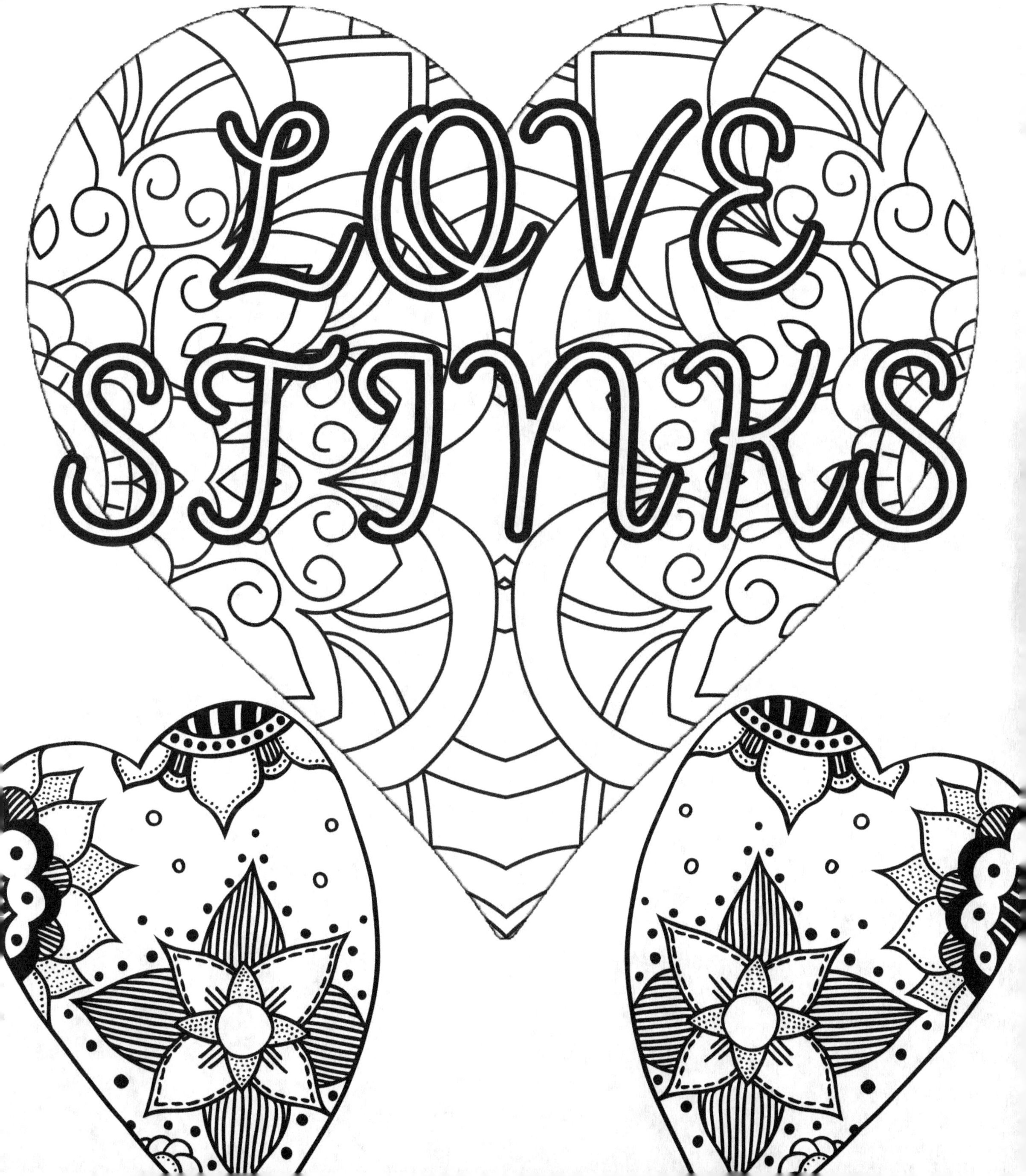

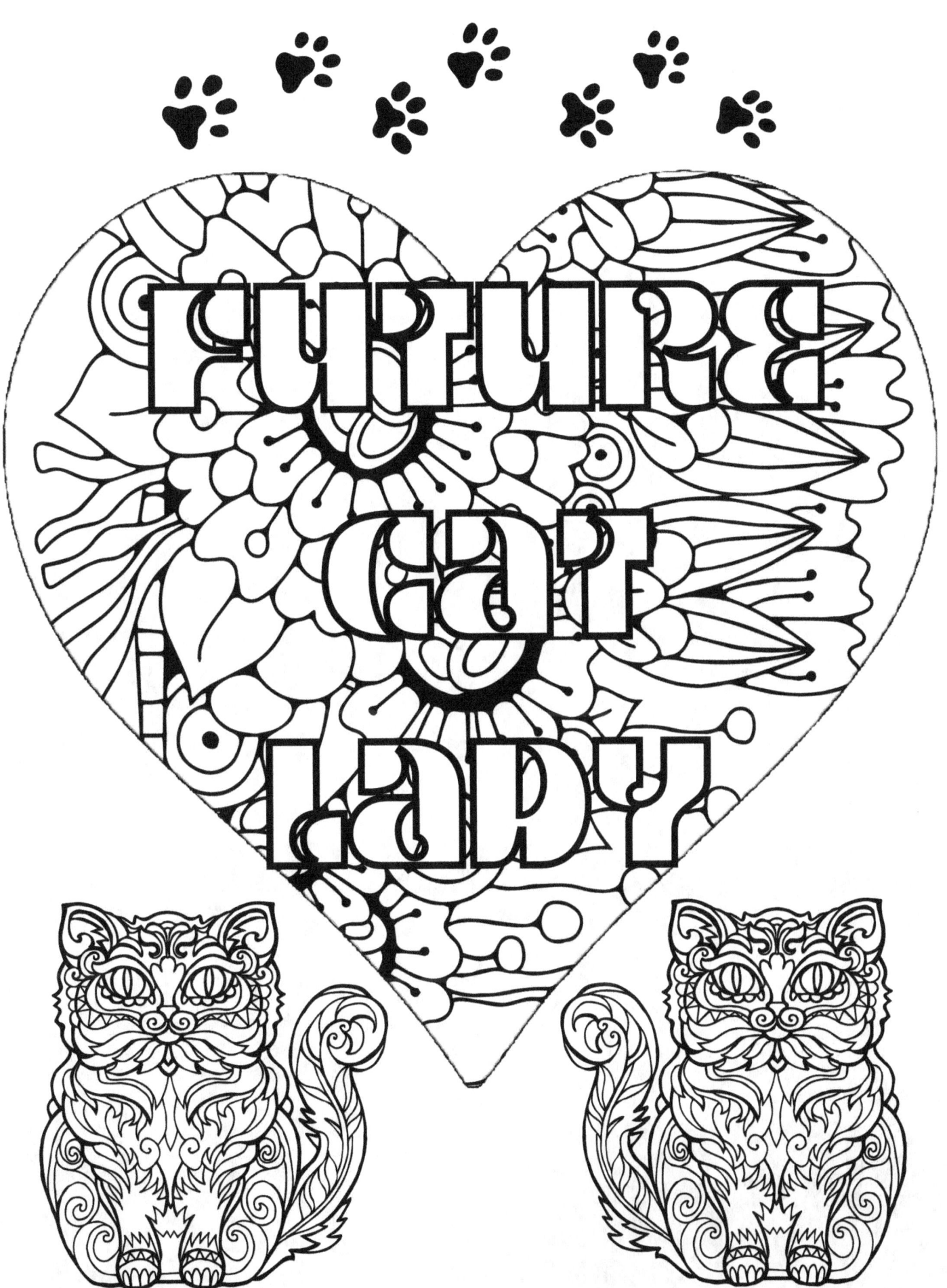

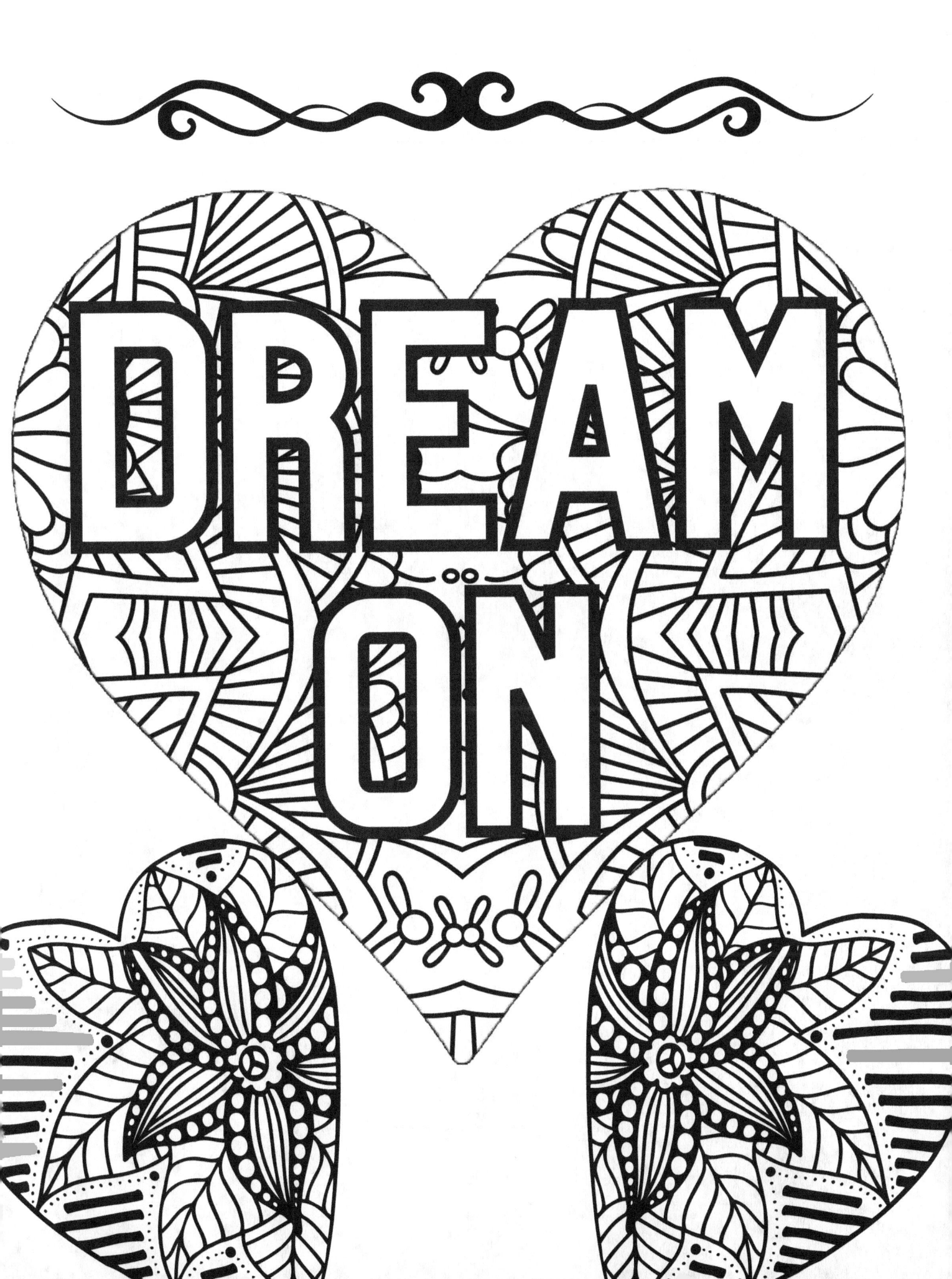

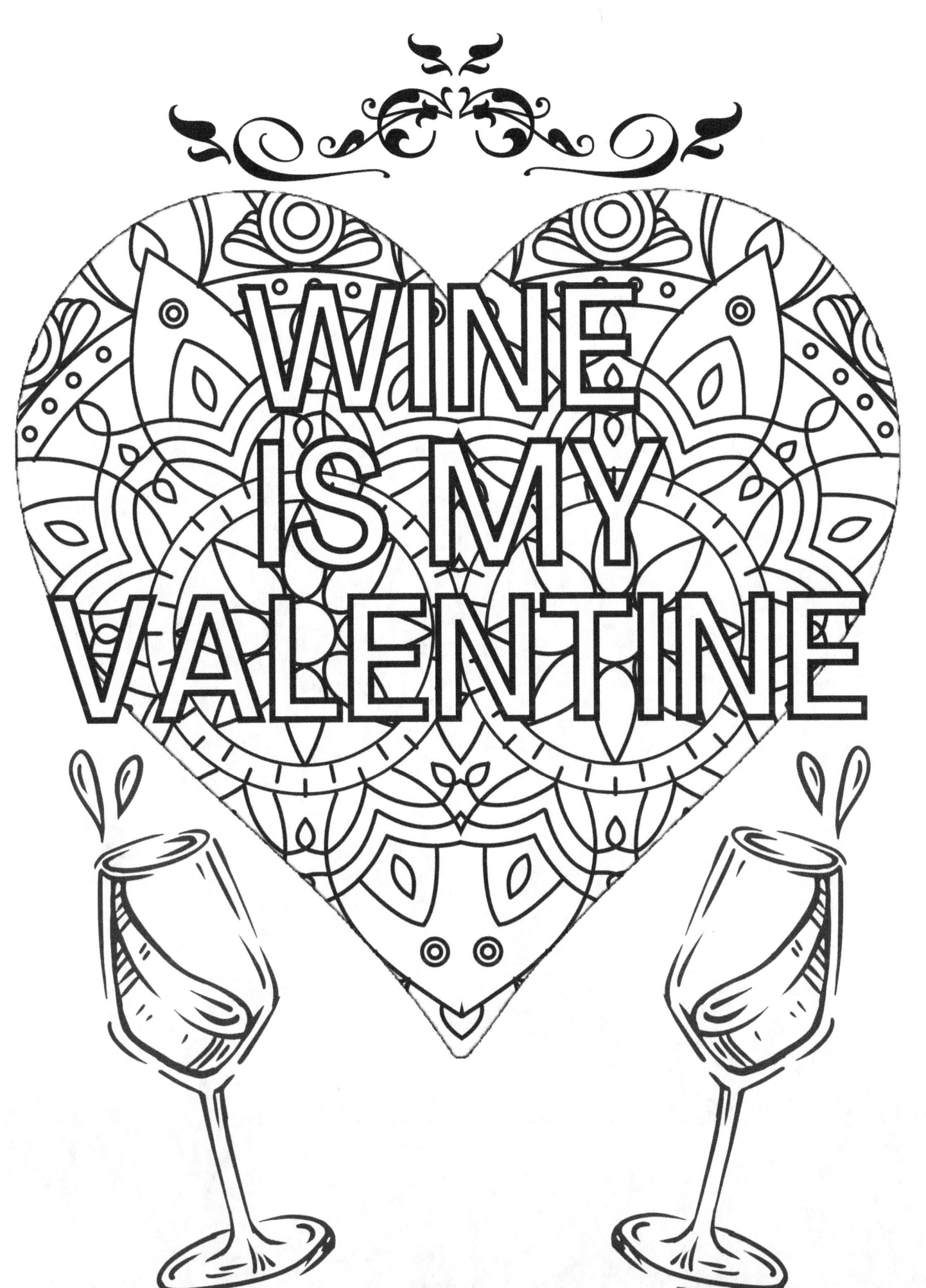

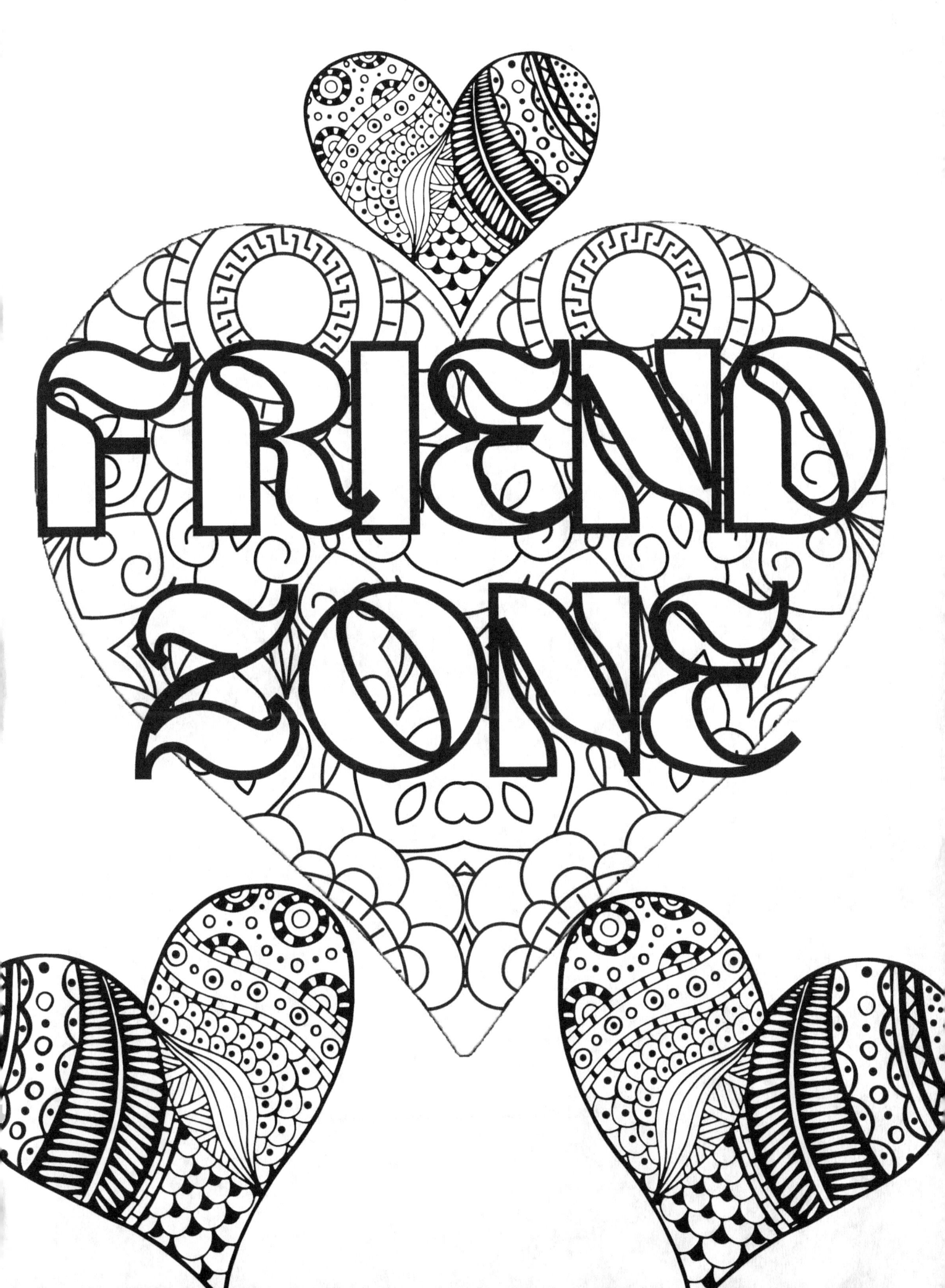

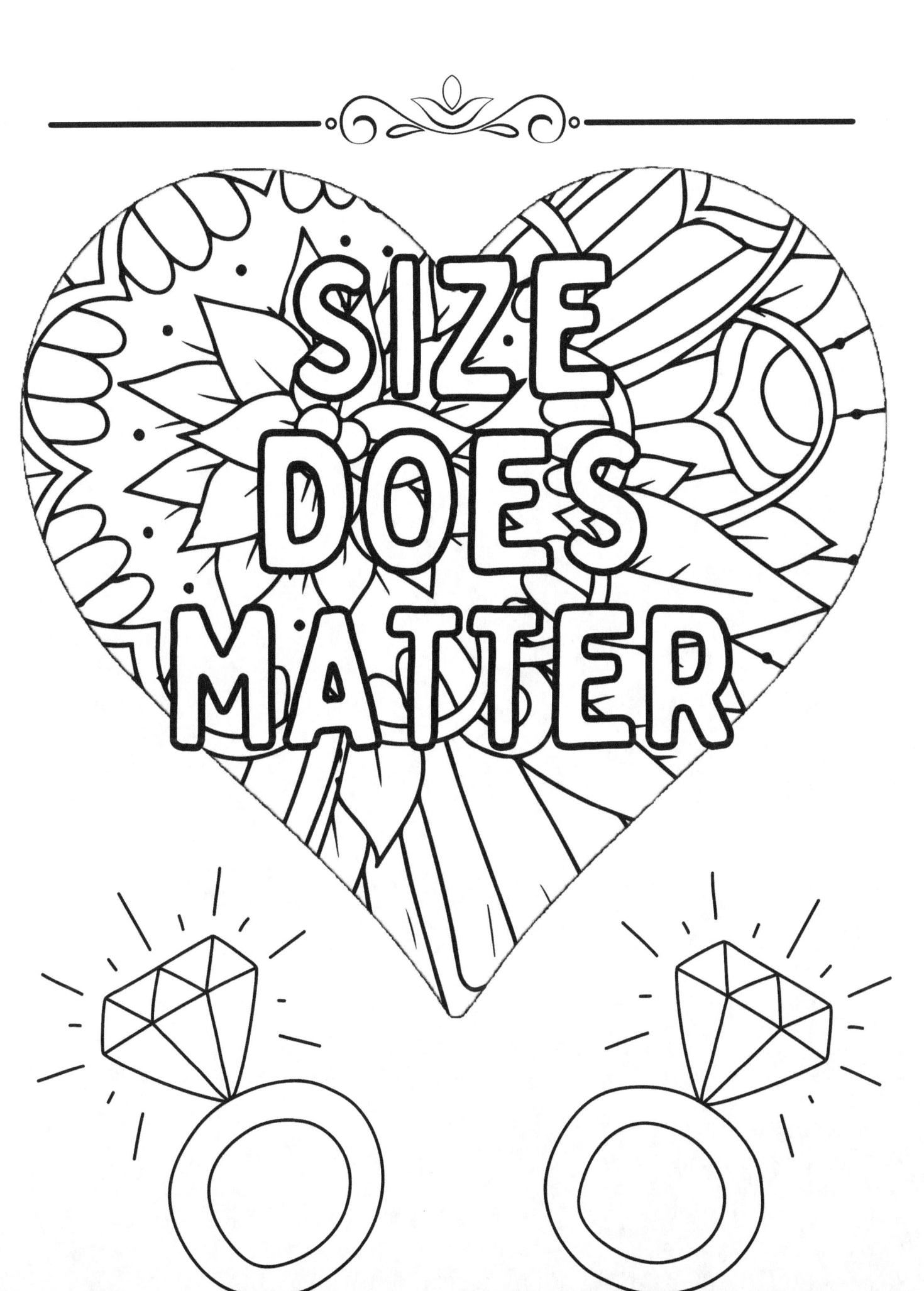

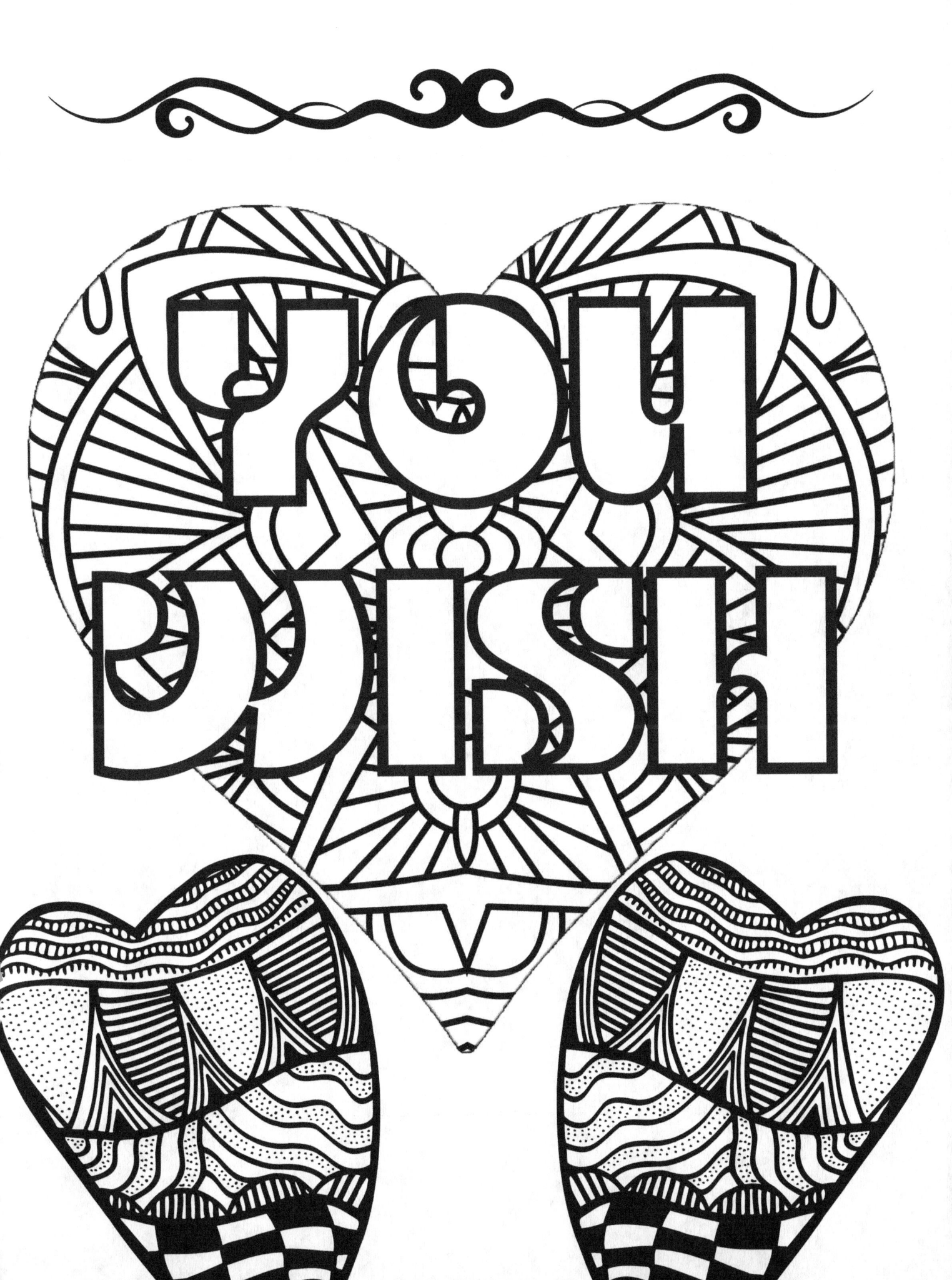

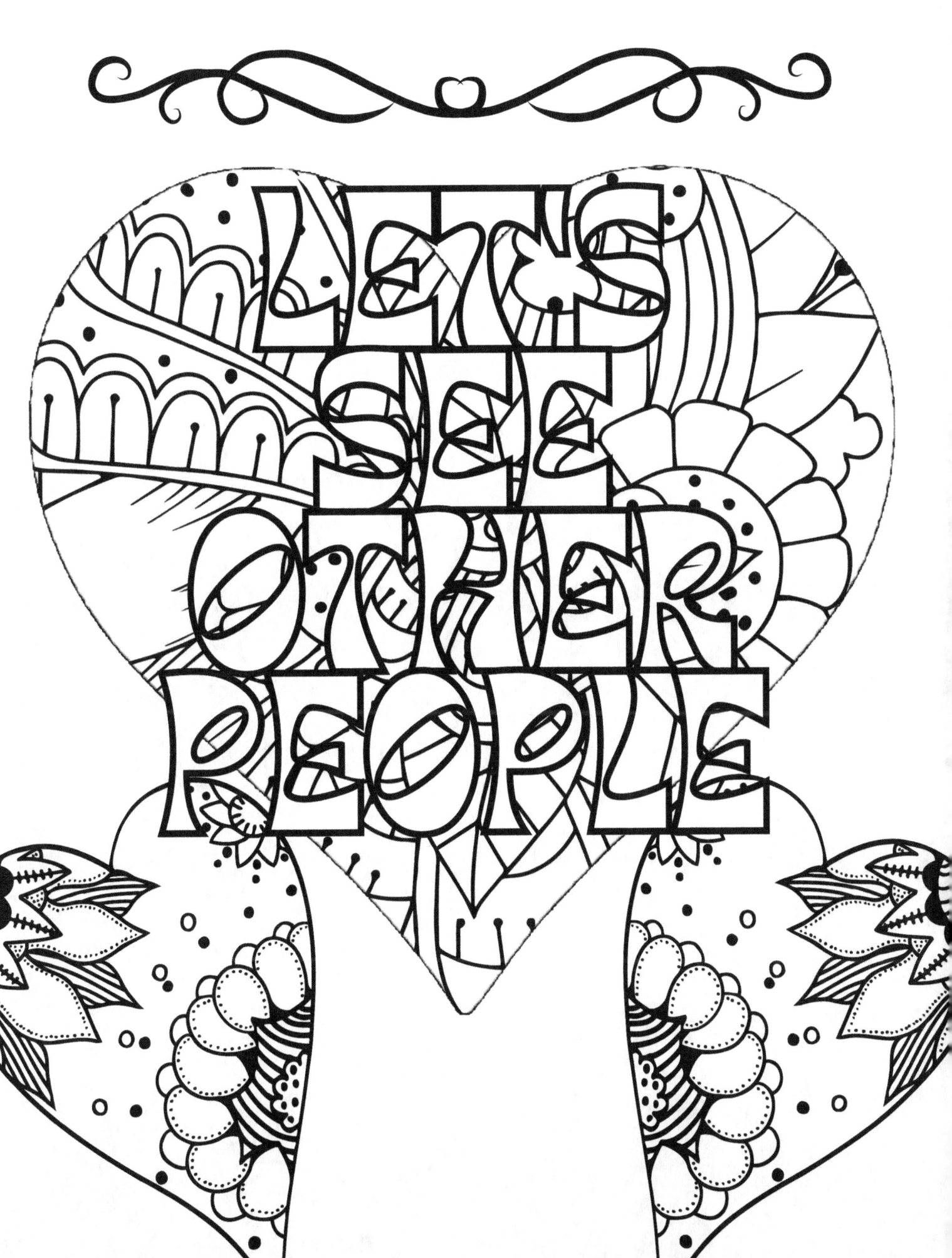

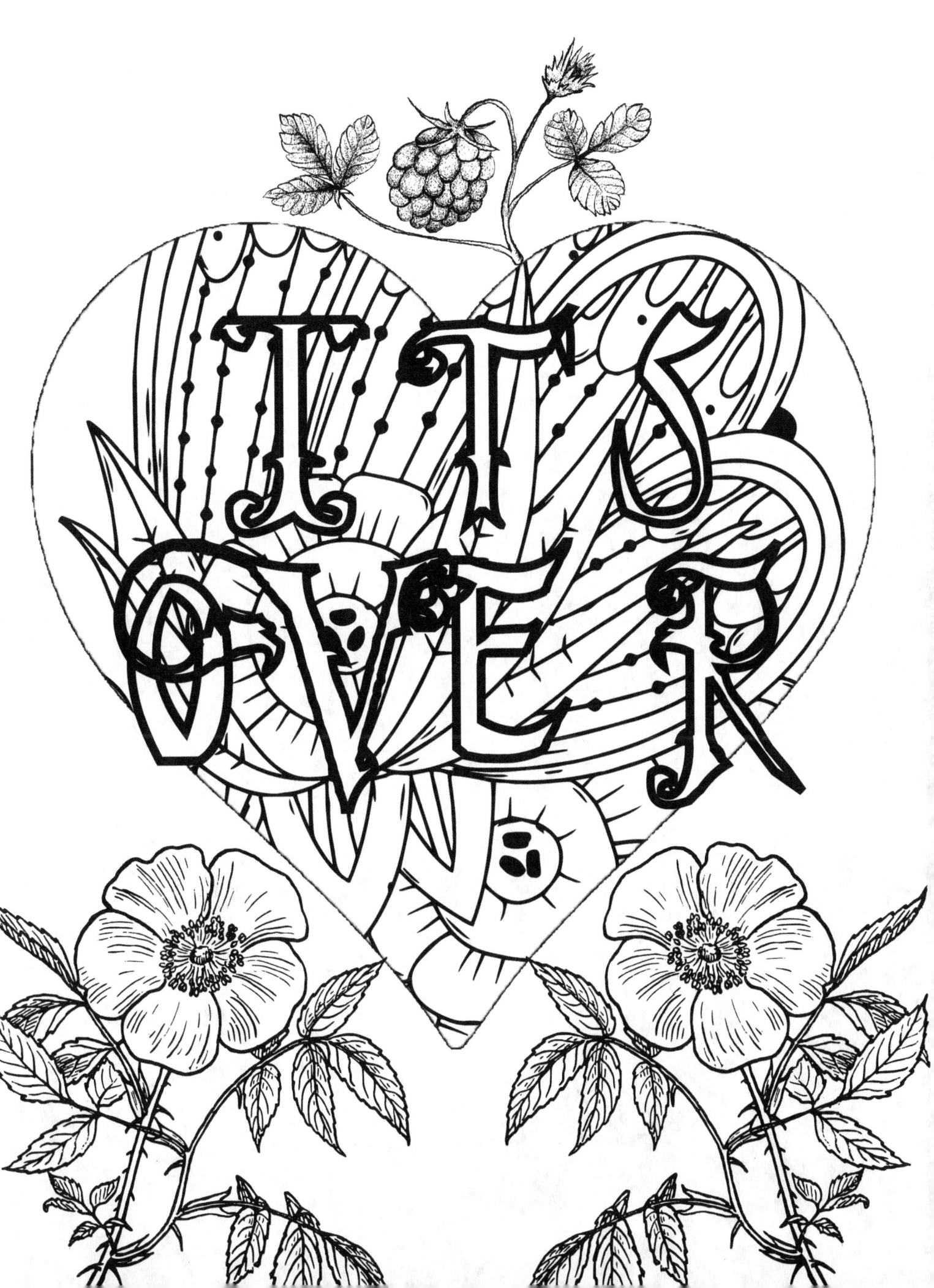

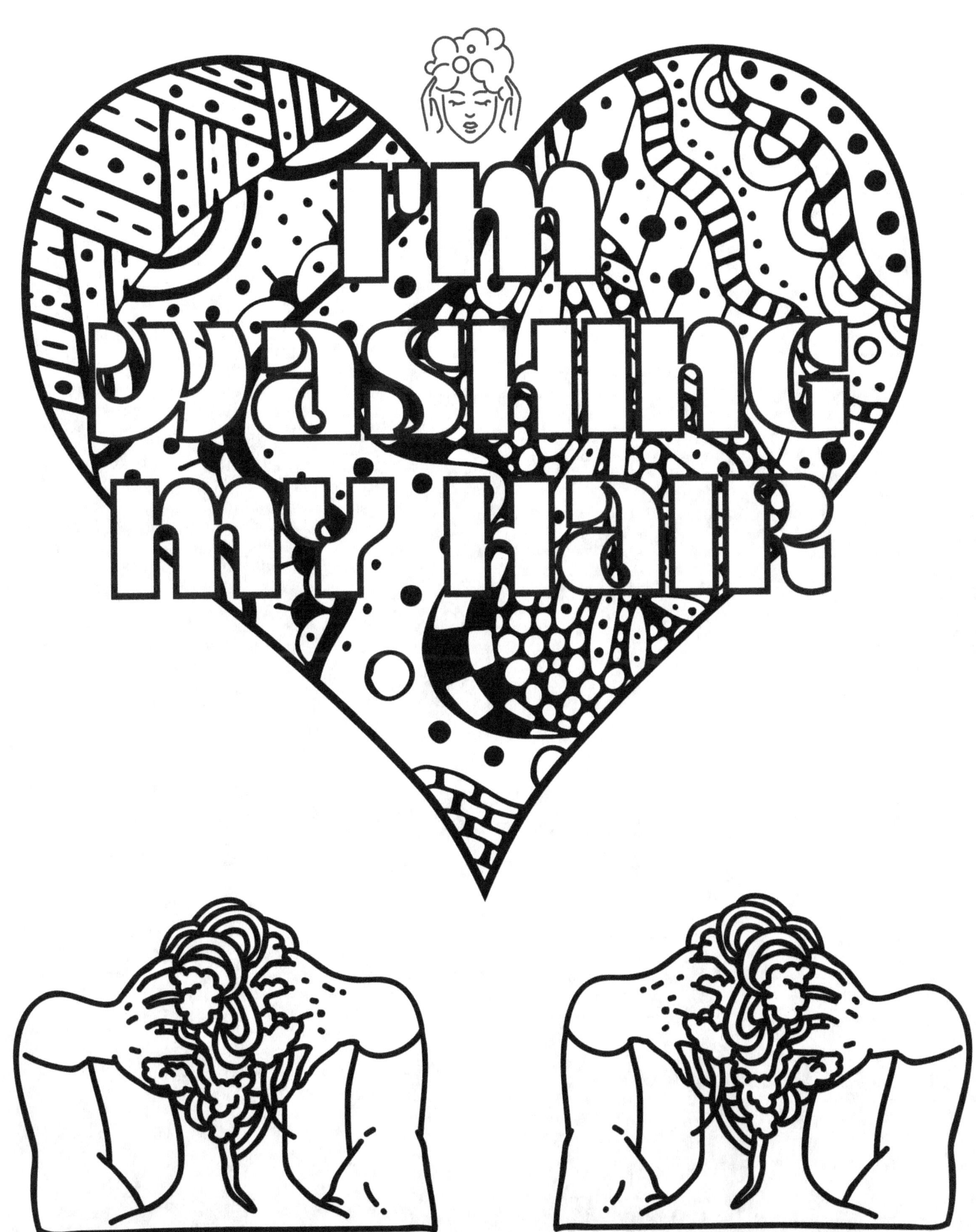

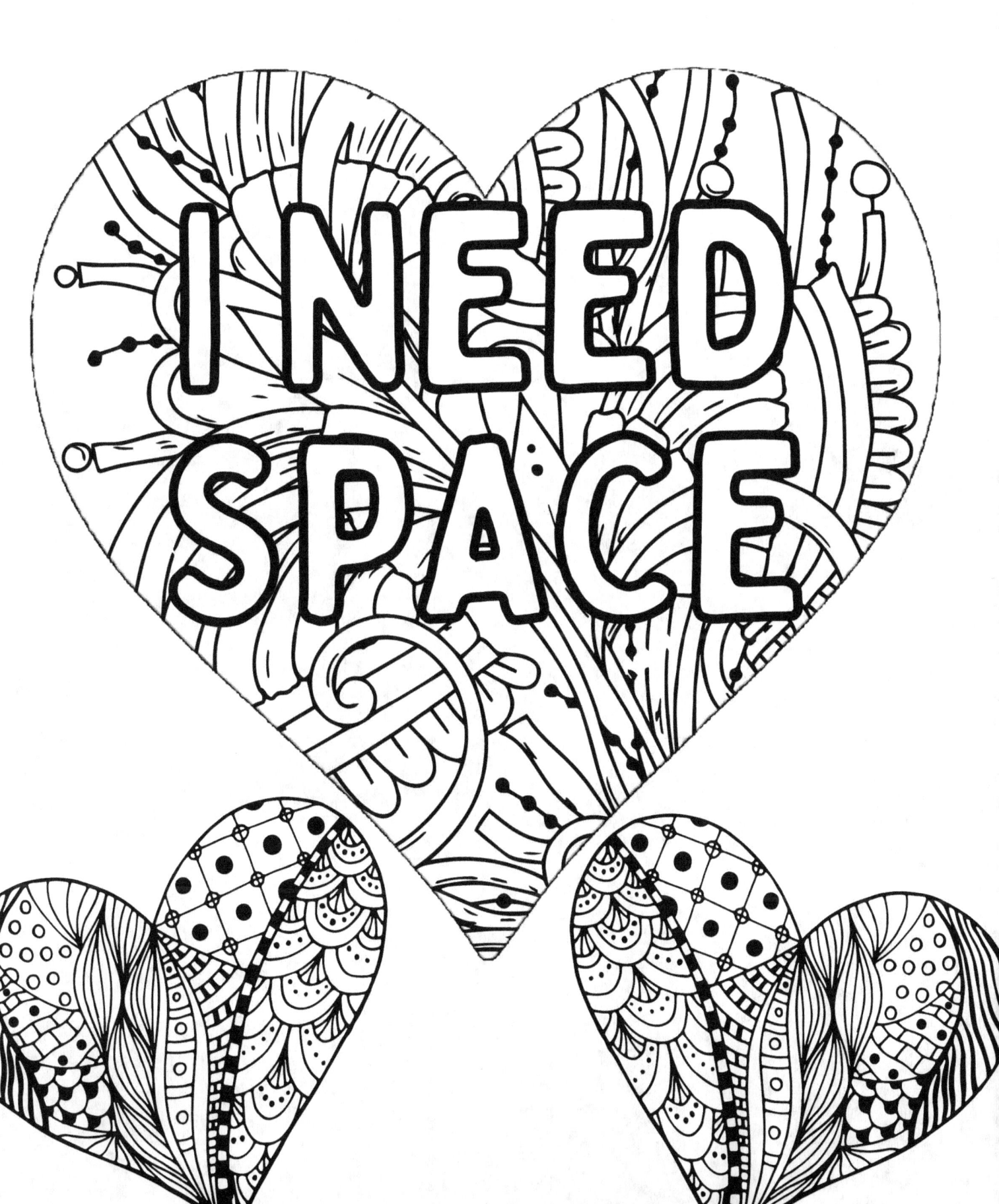

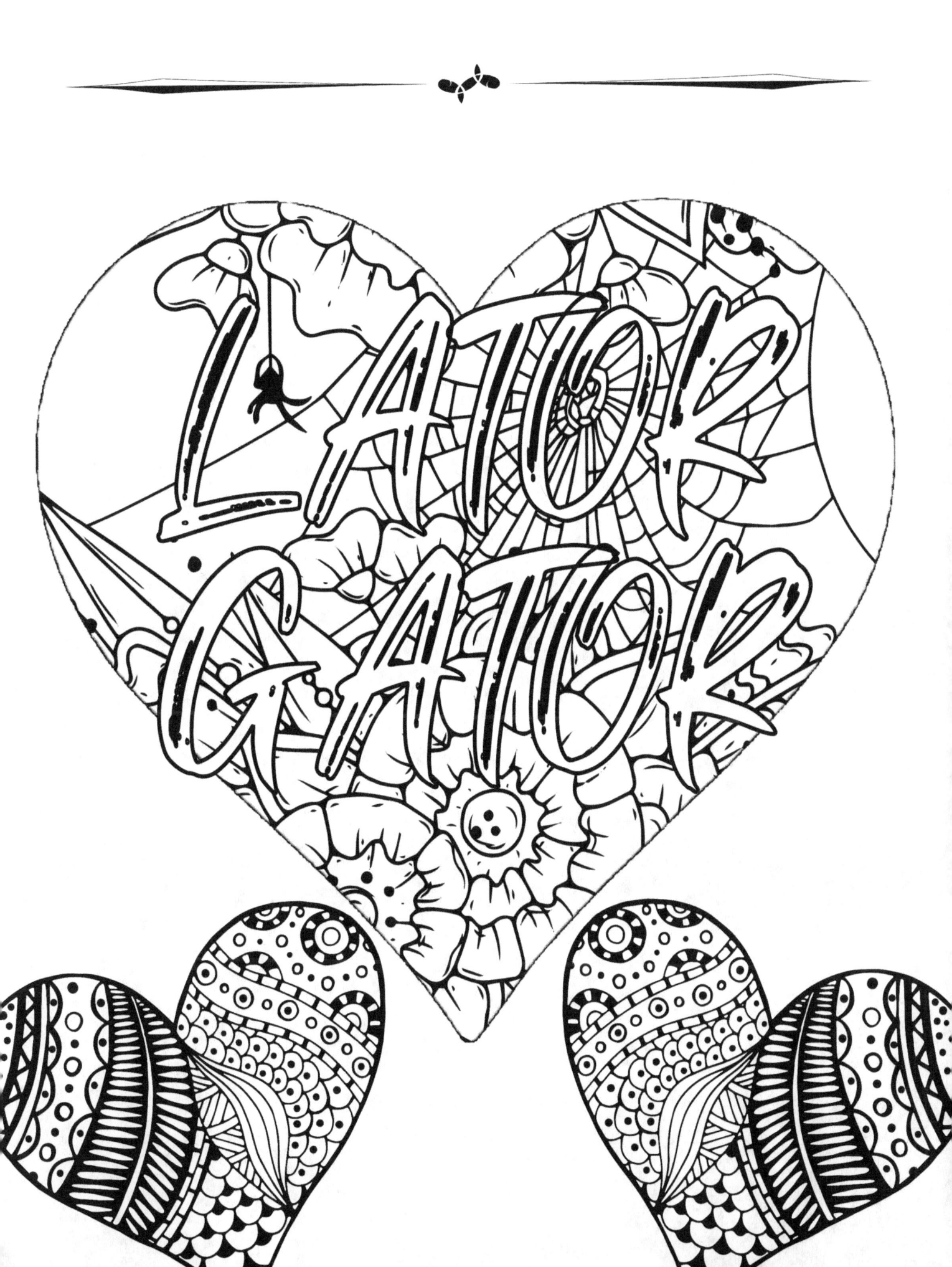

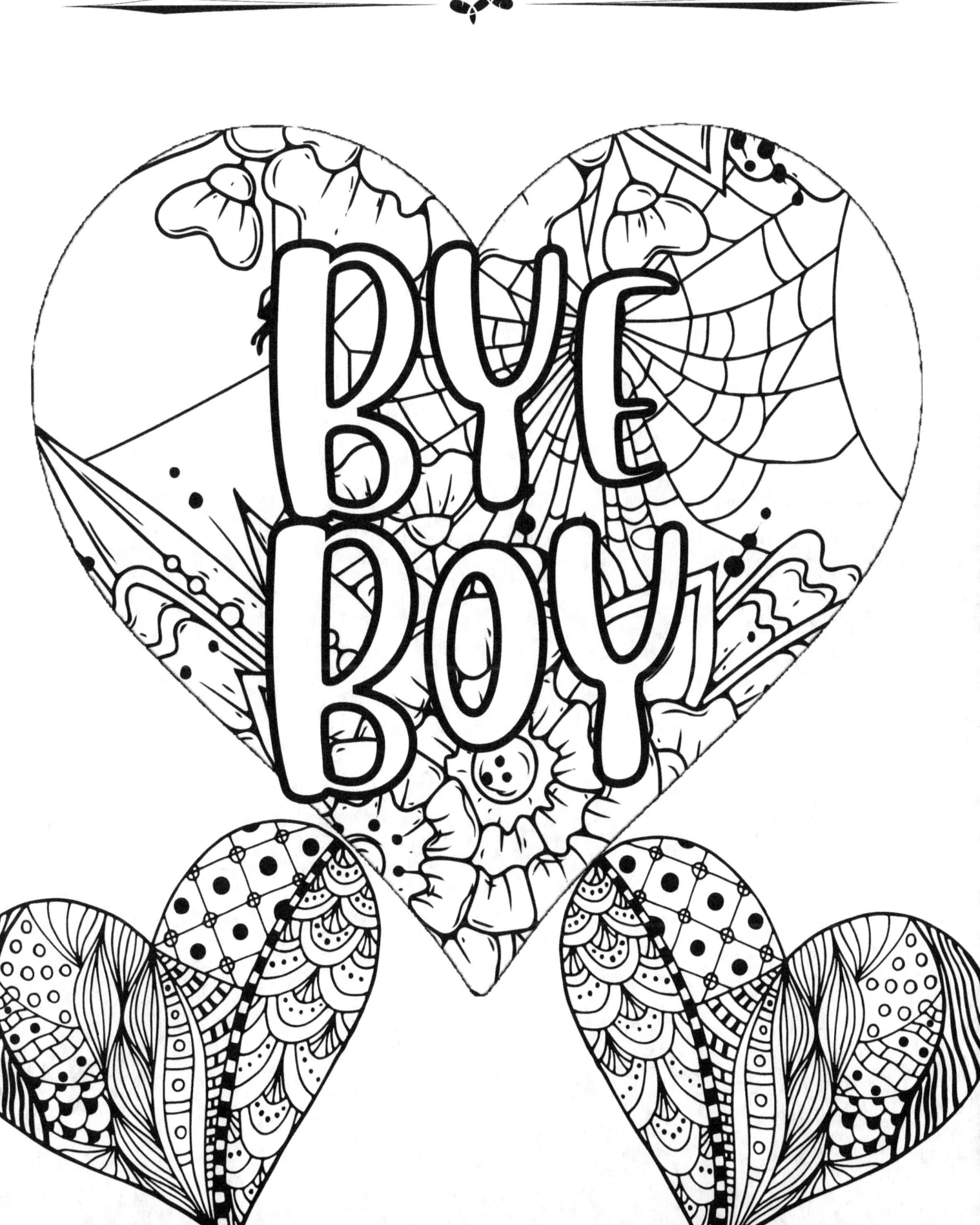

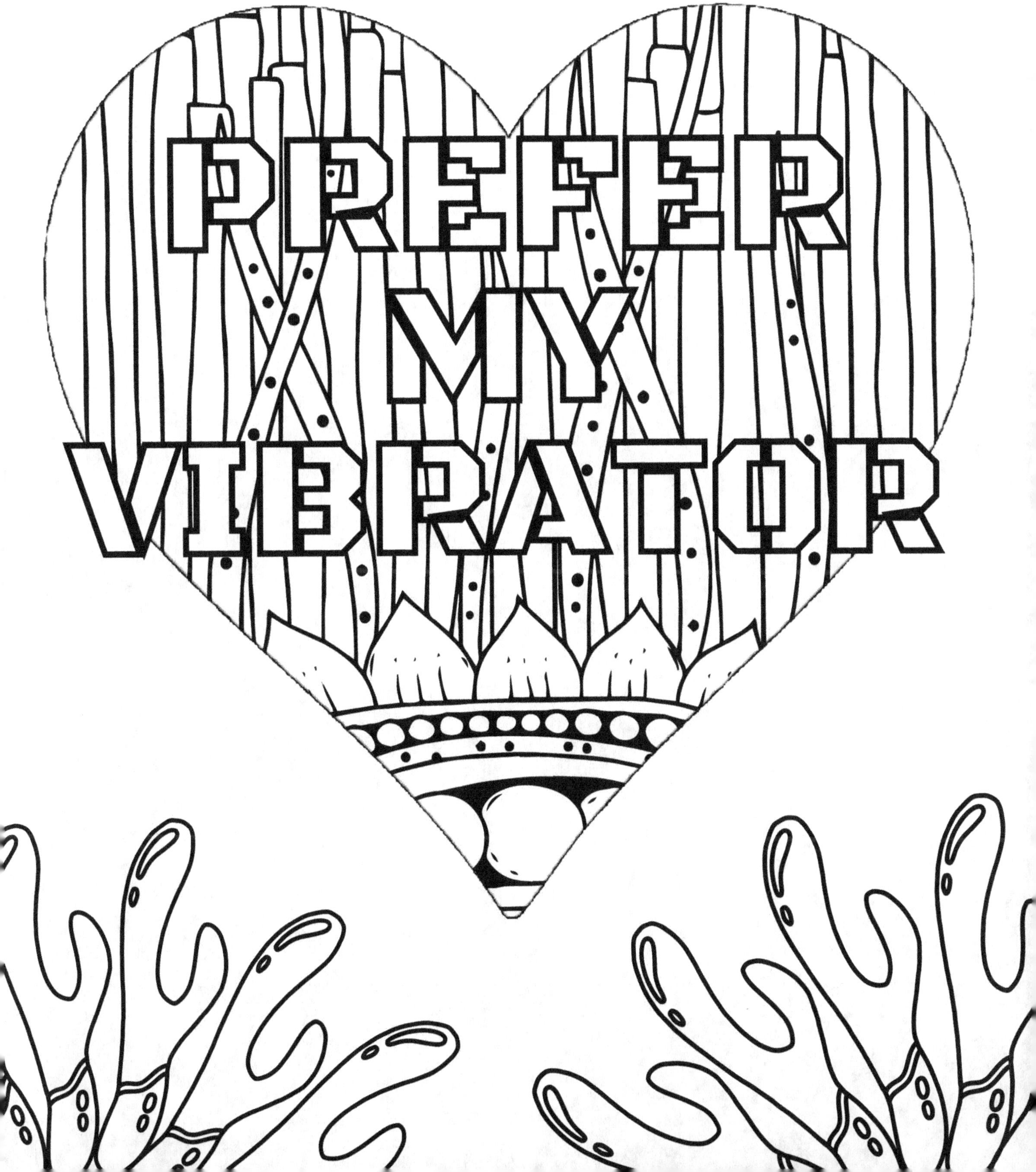

PREFER MY VIBRATOR

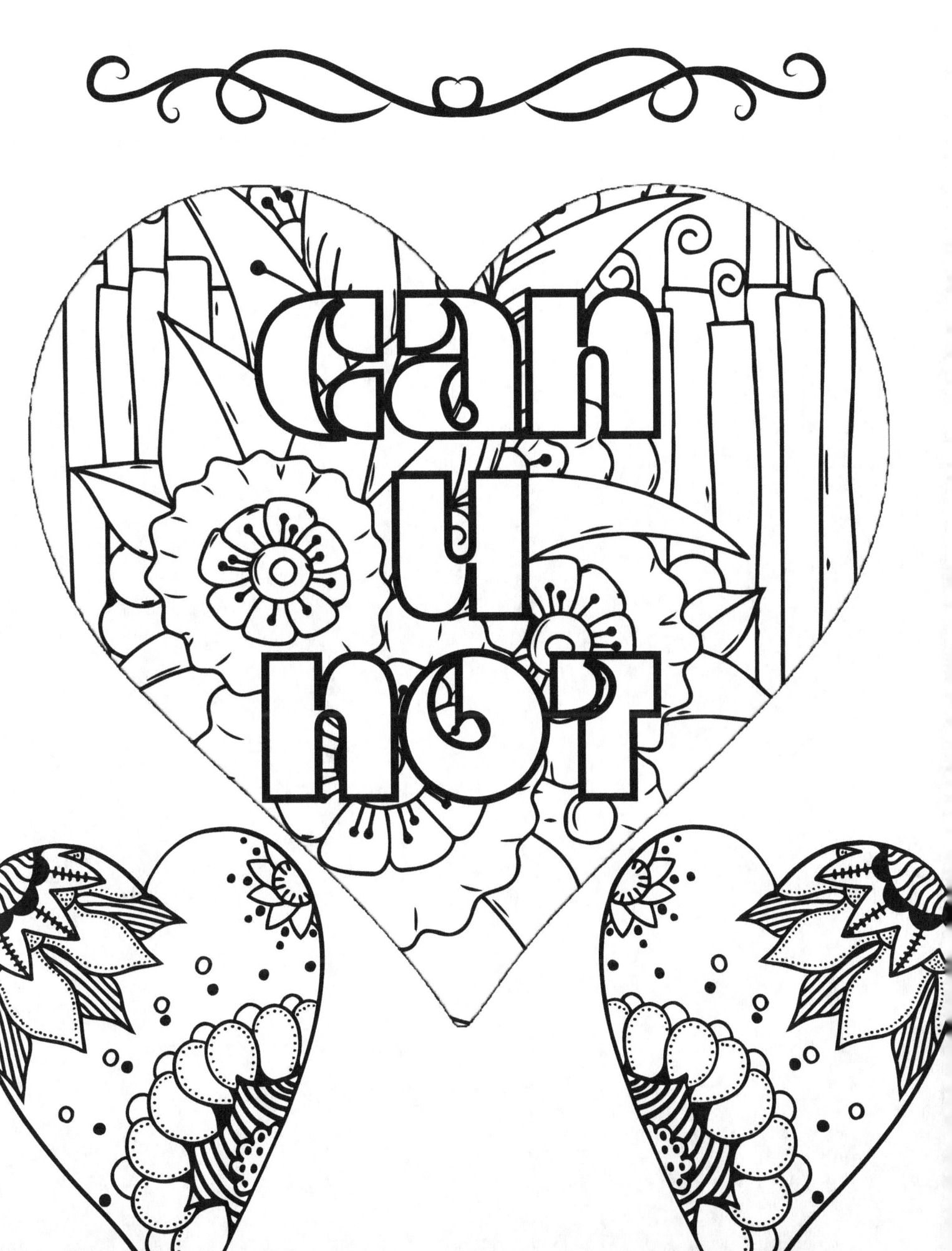

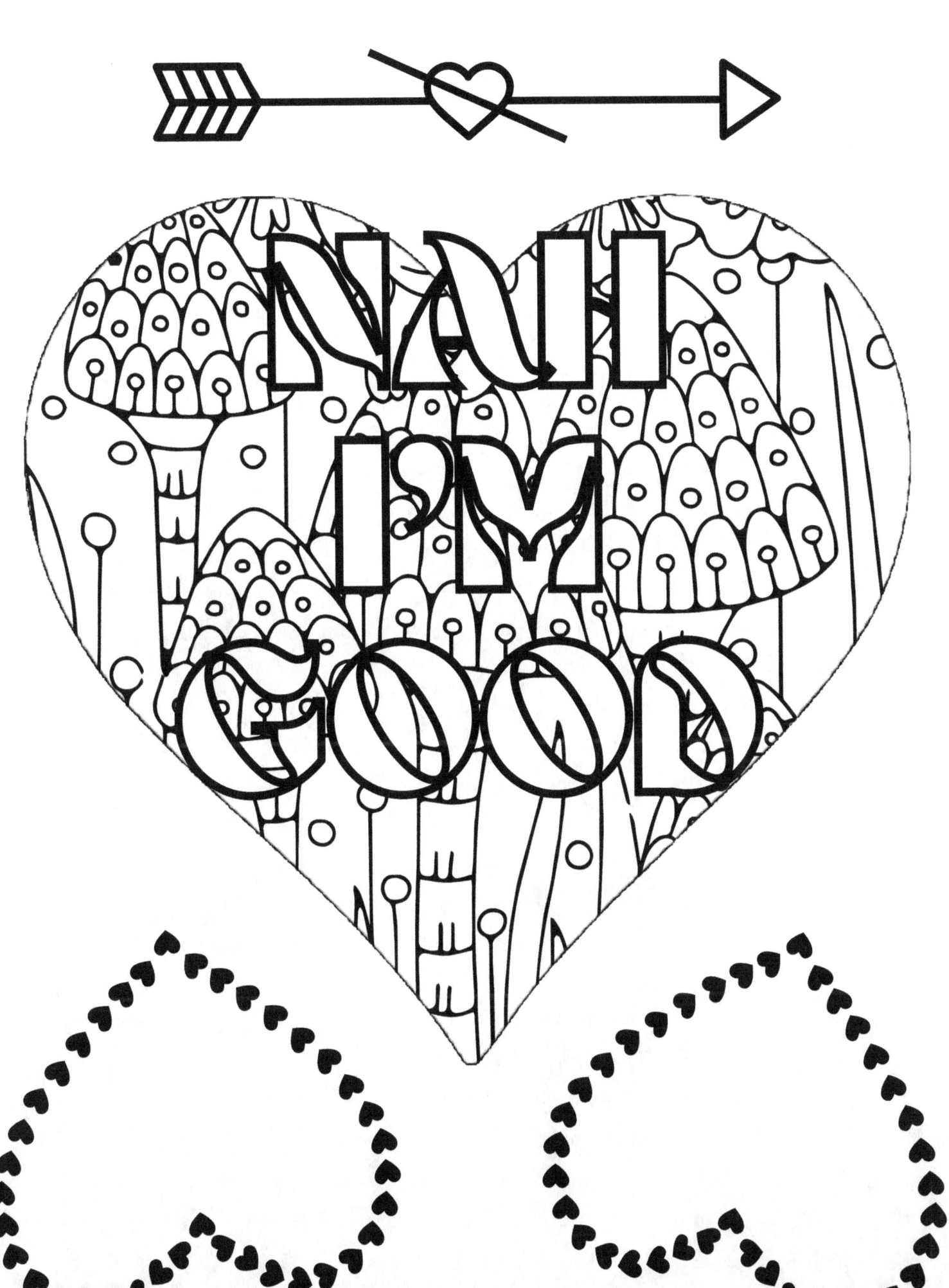

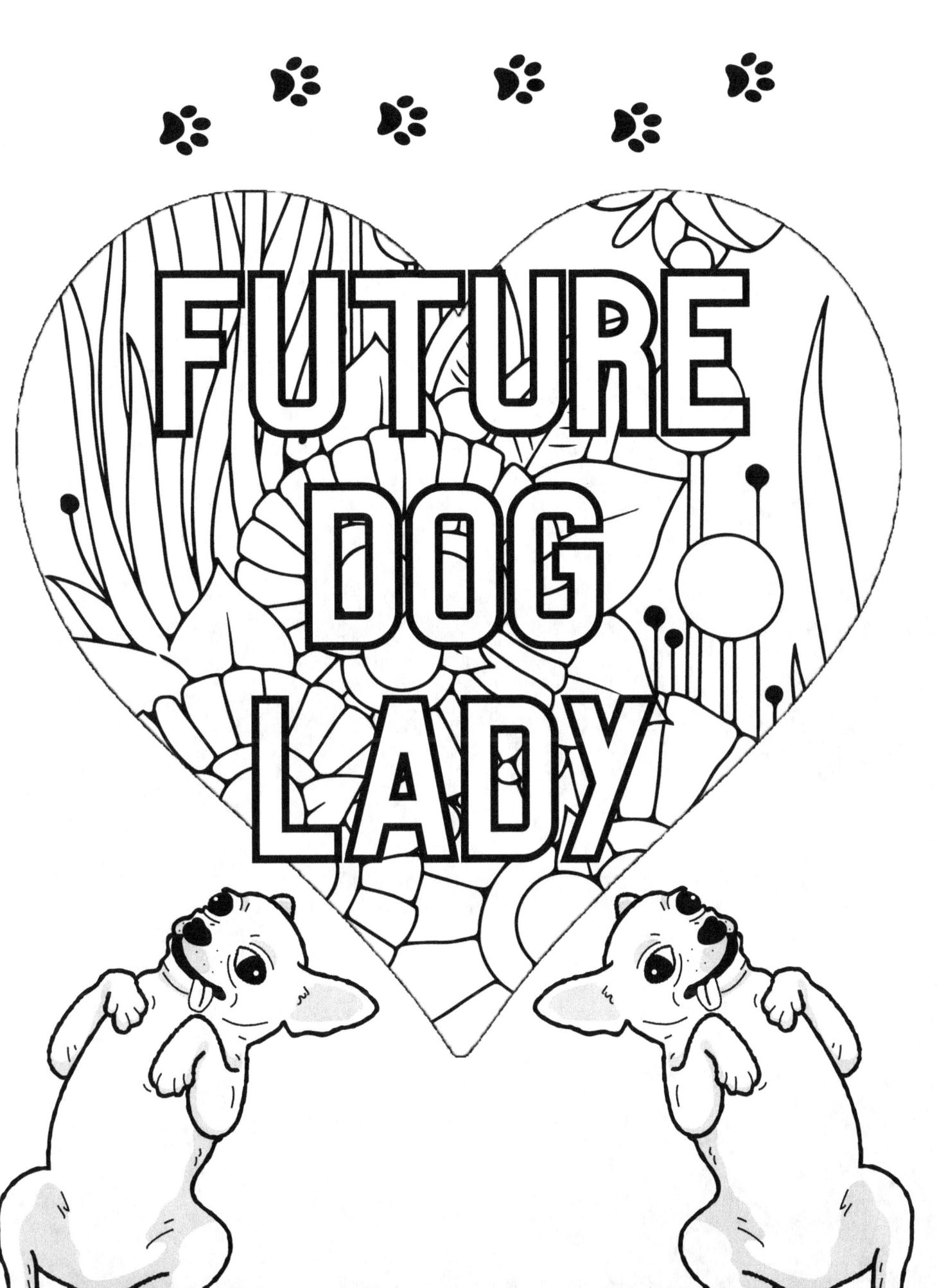

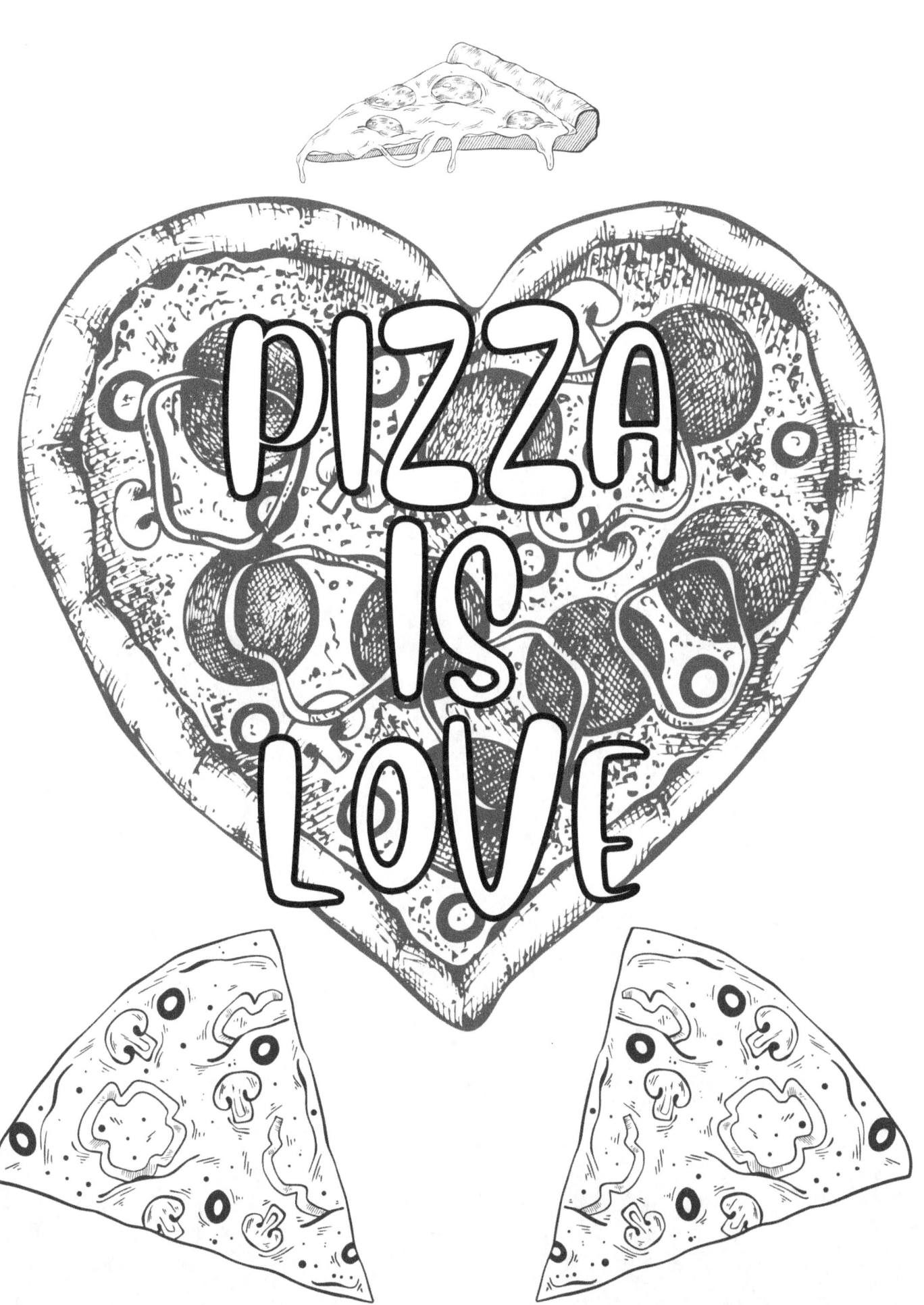

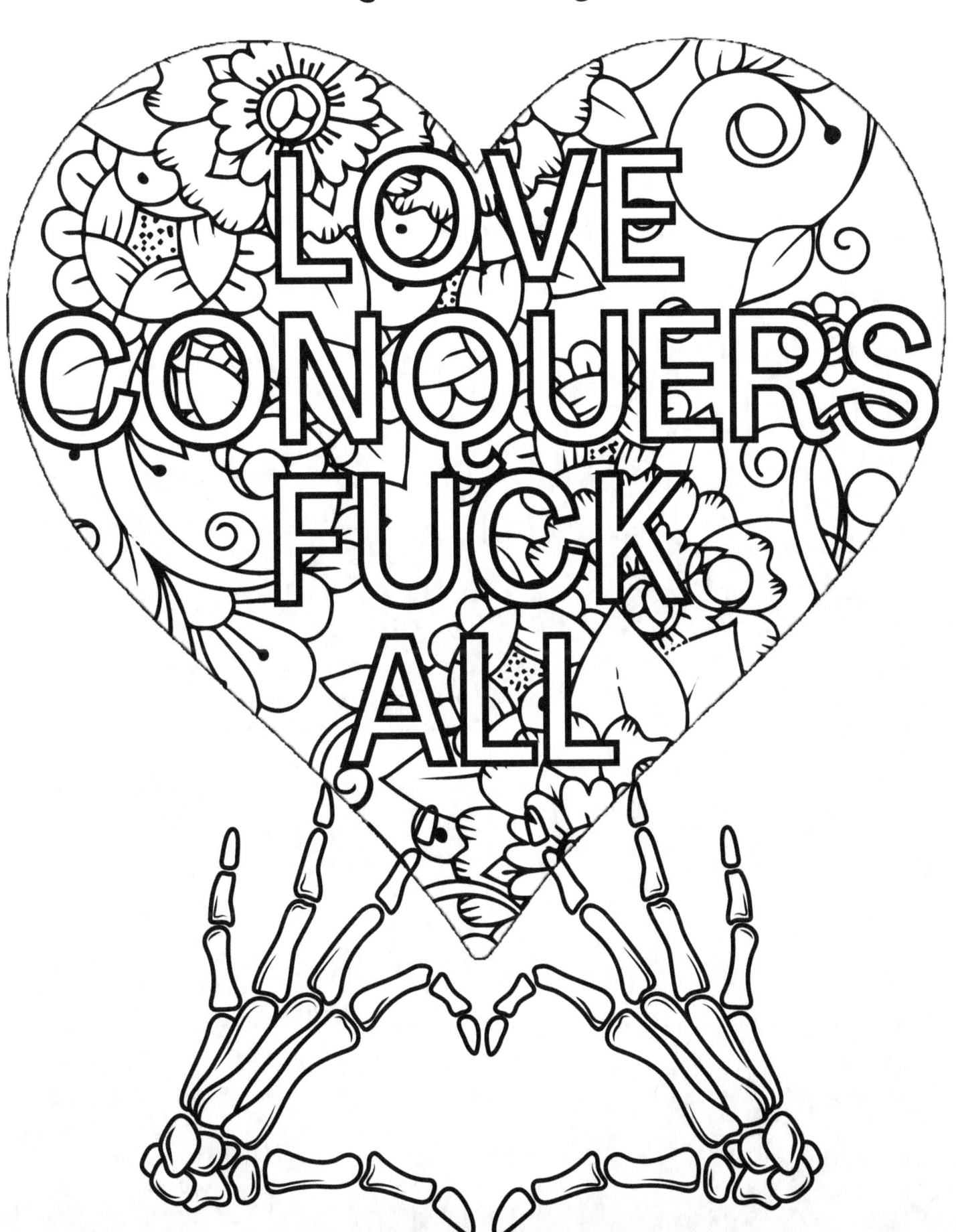

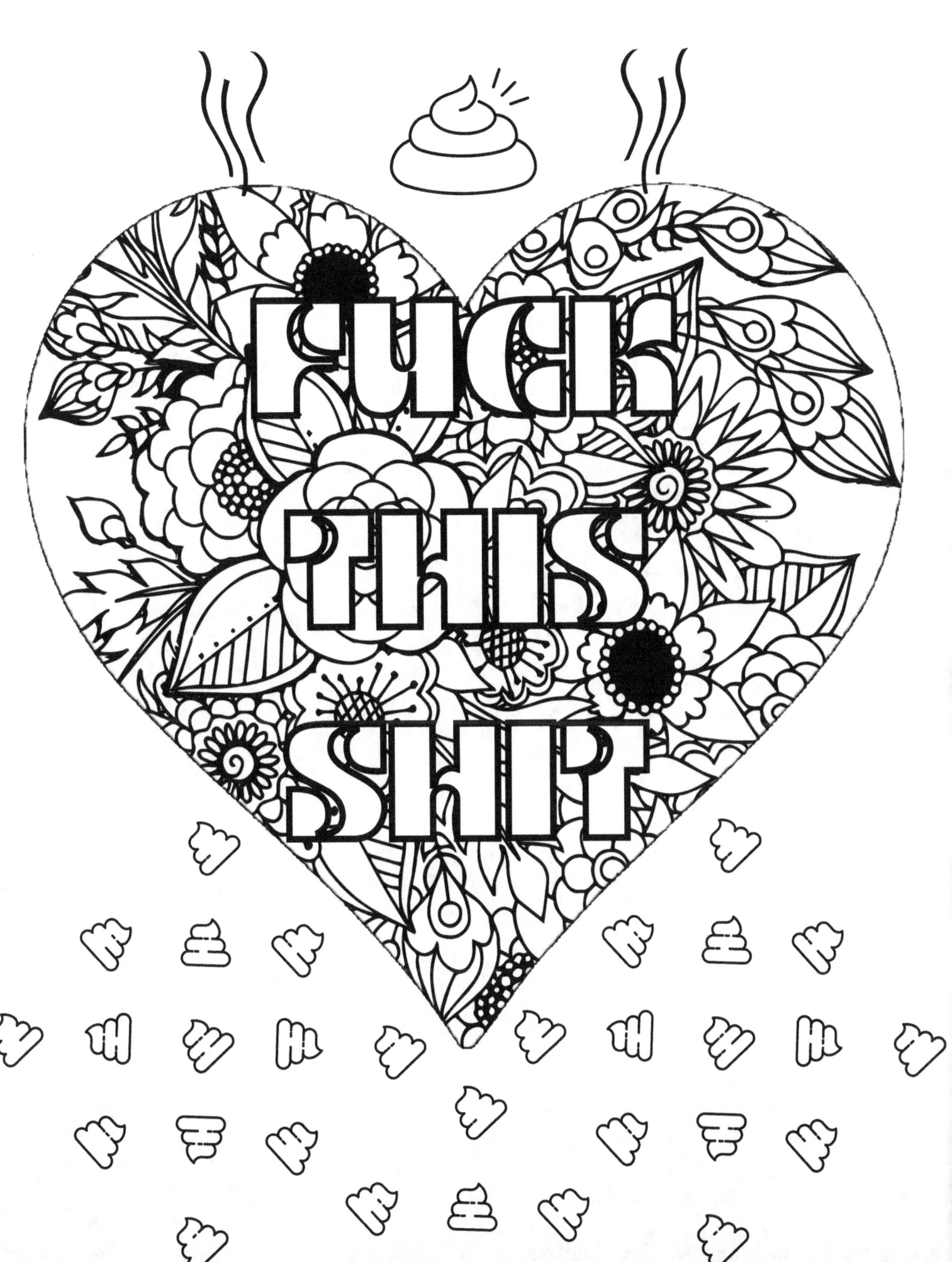

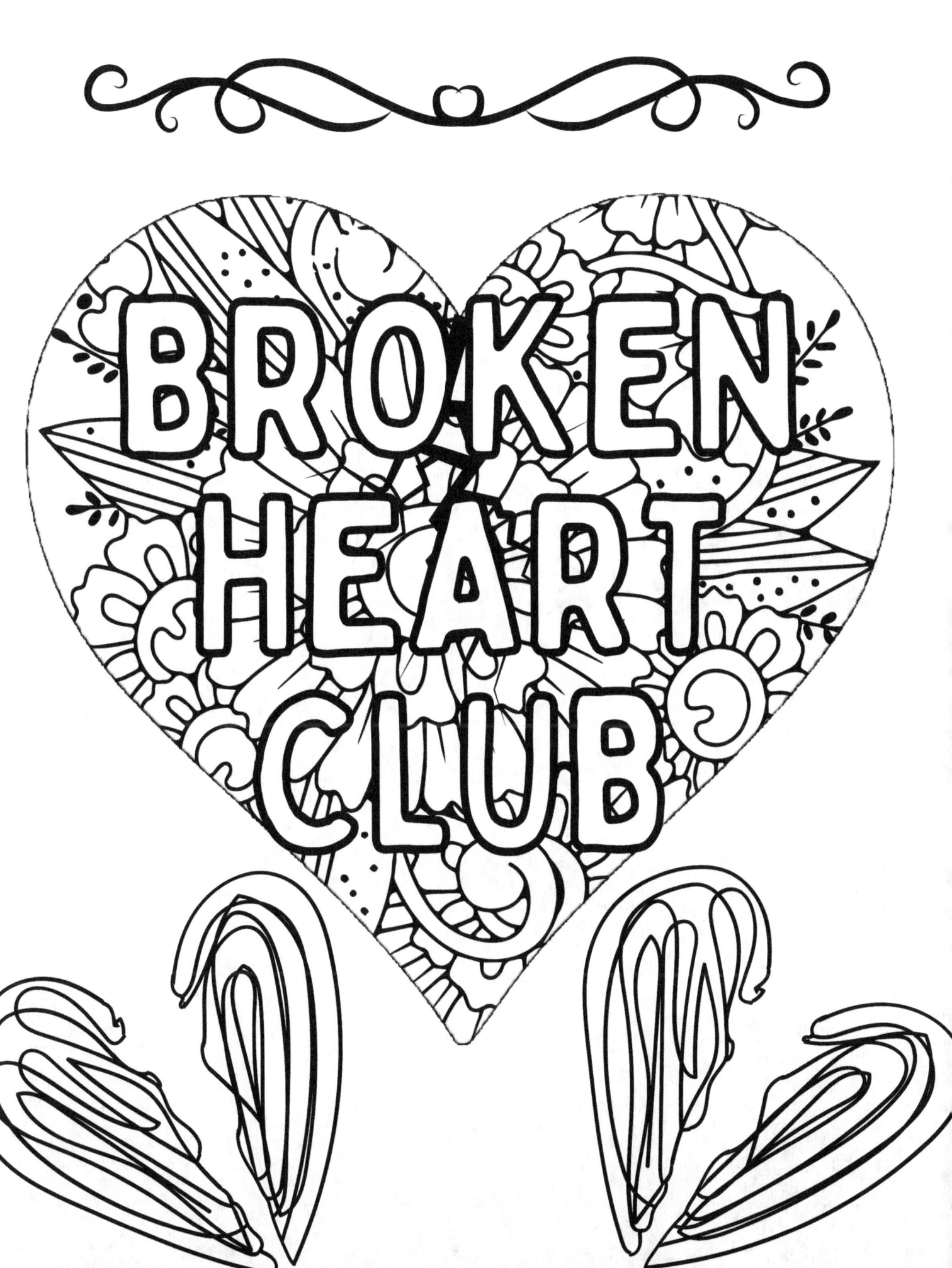

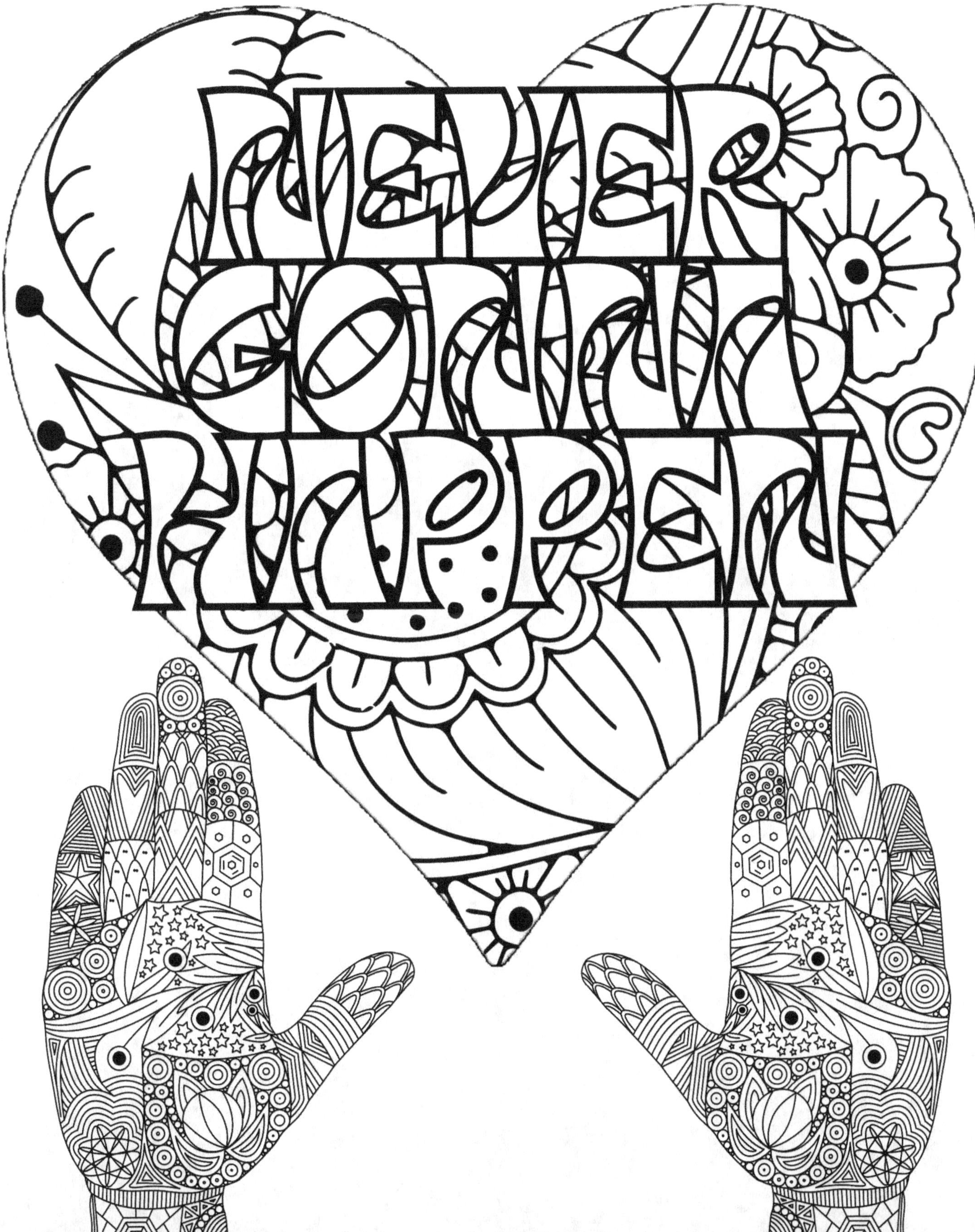

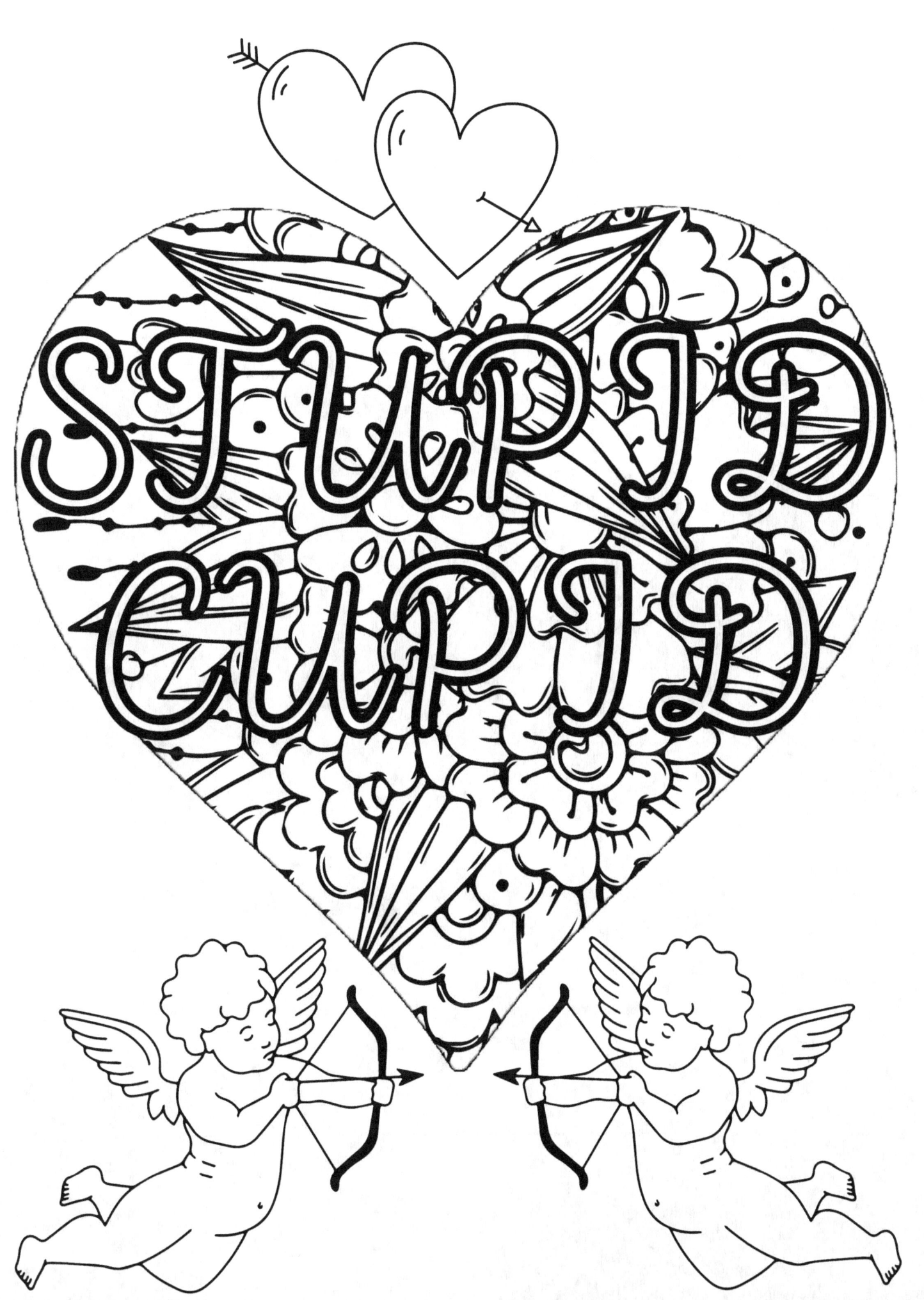

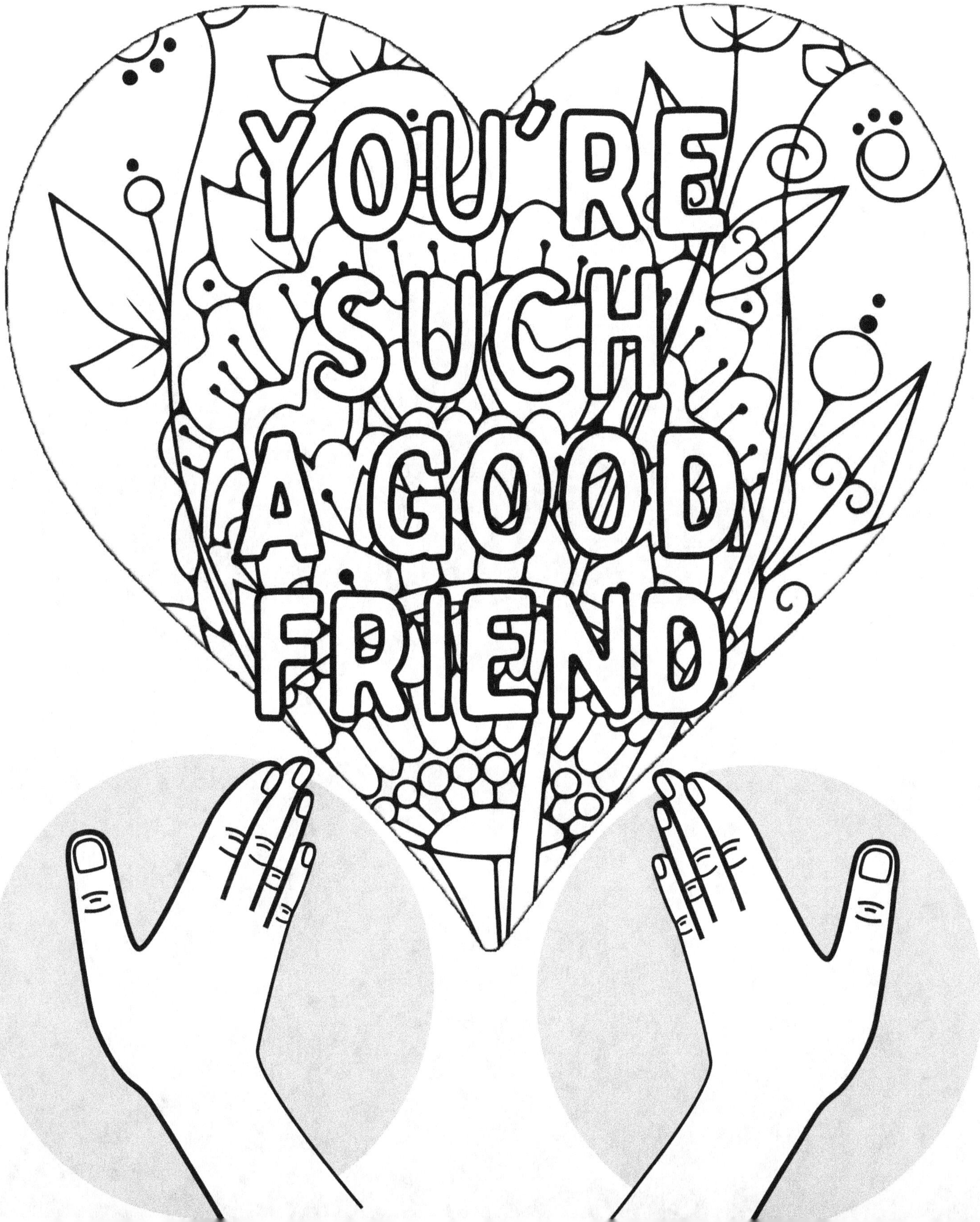

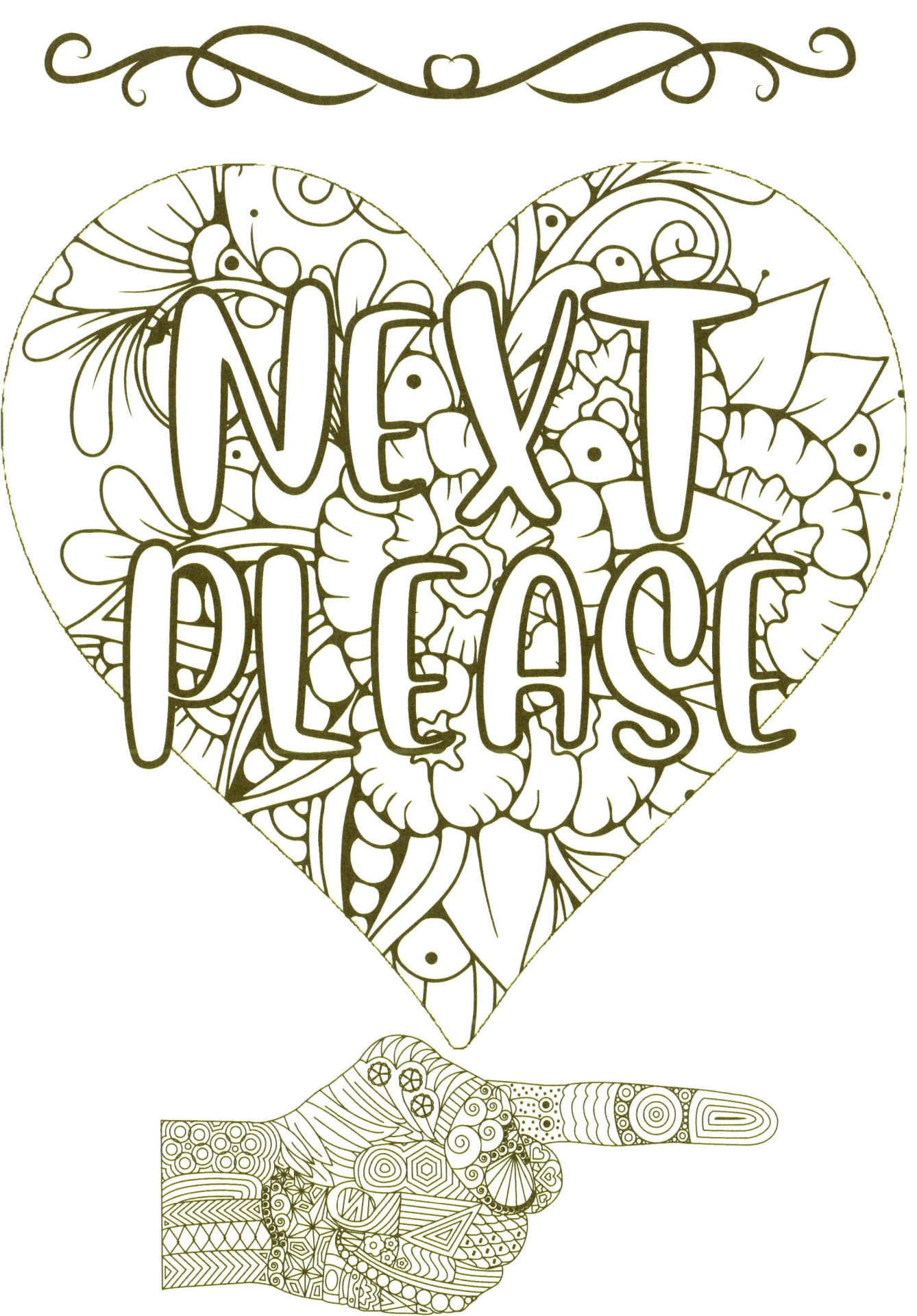

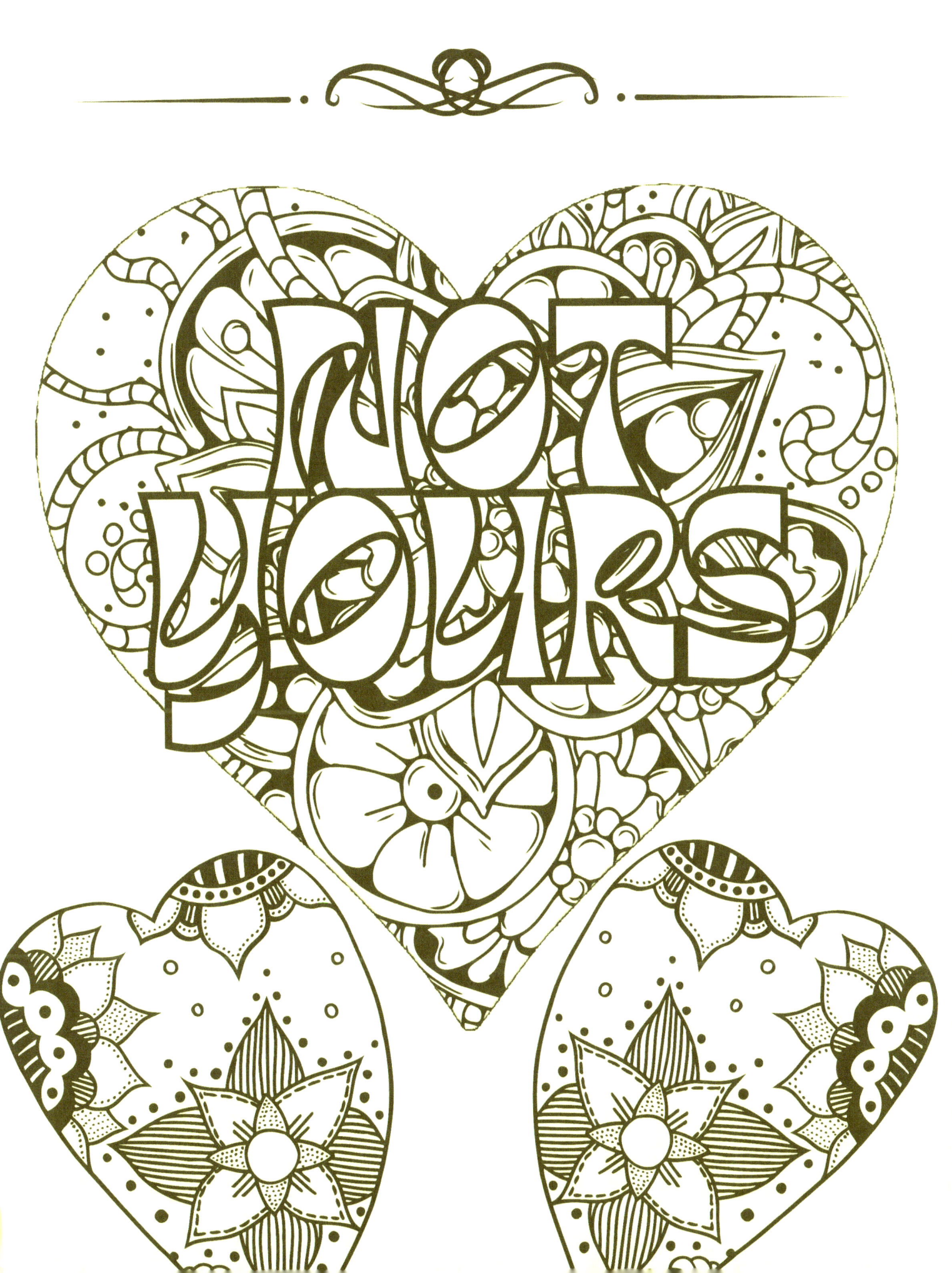

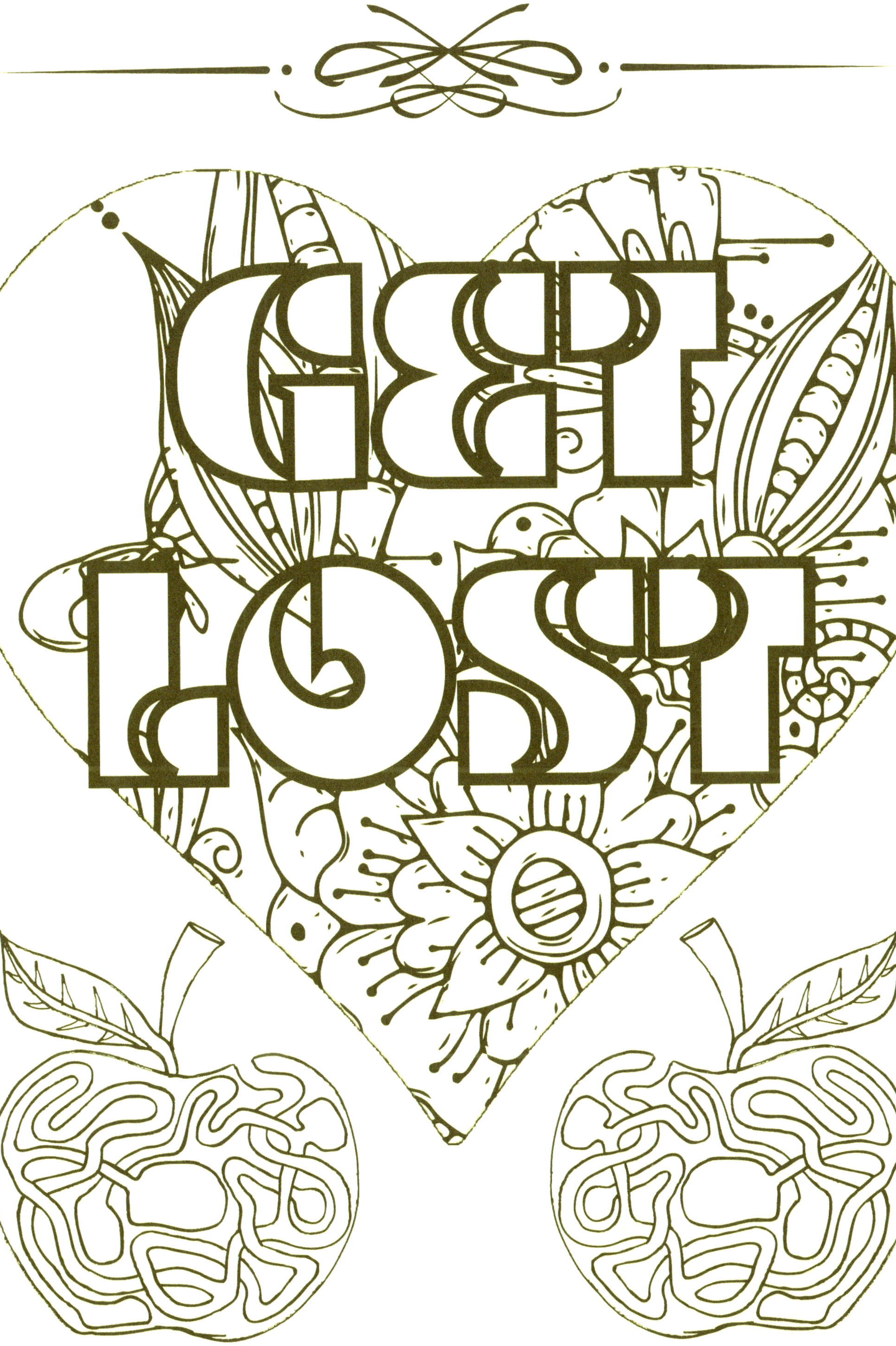

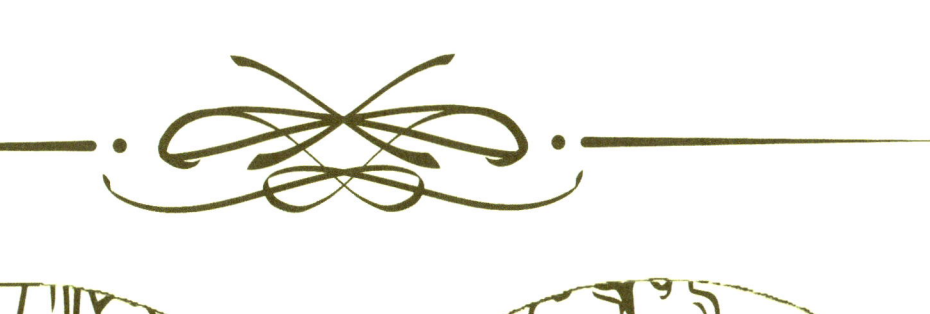

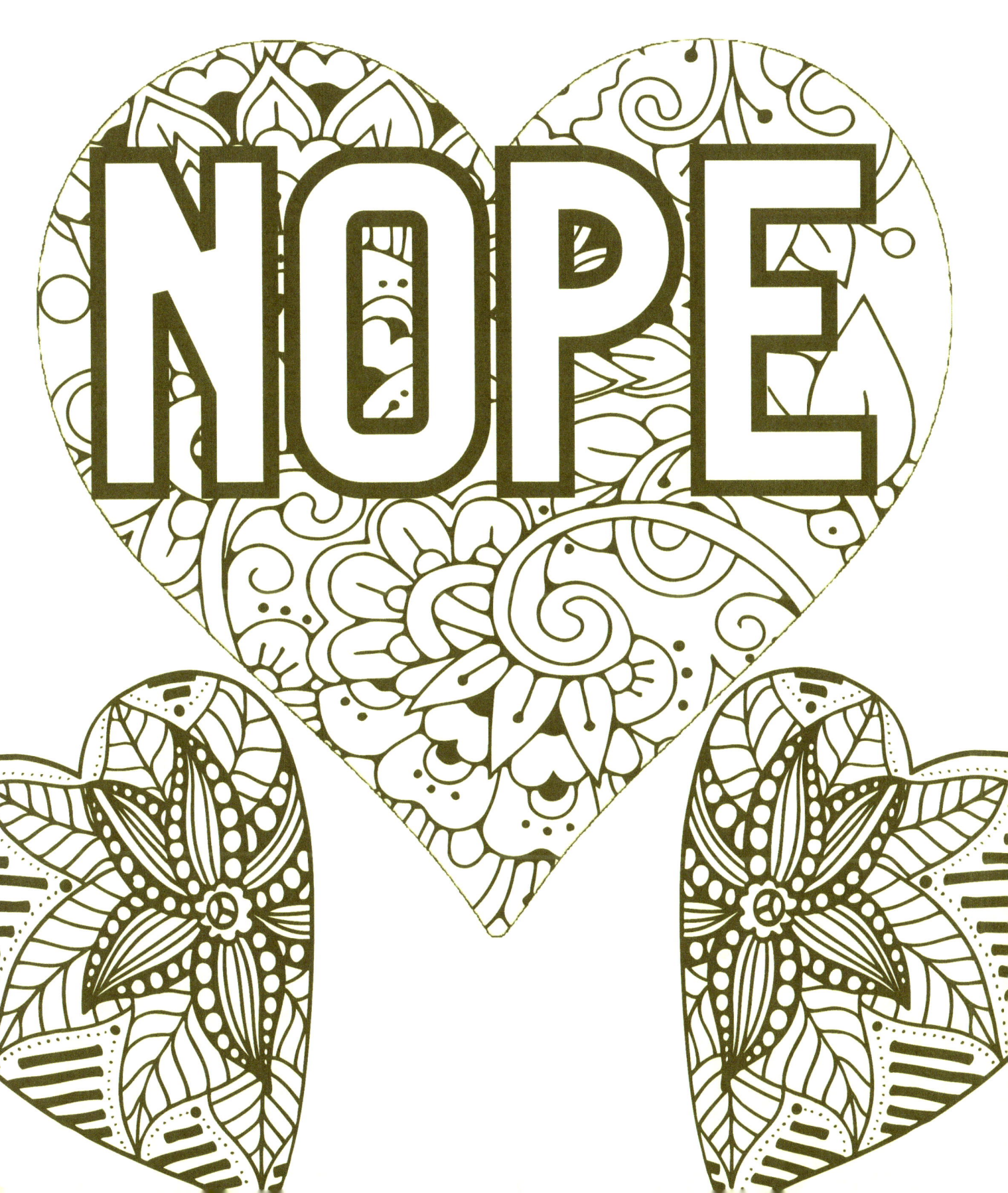

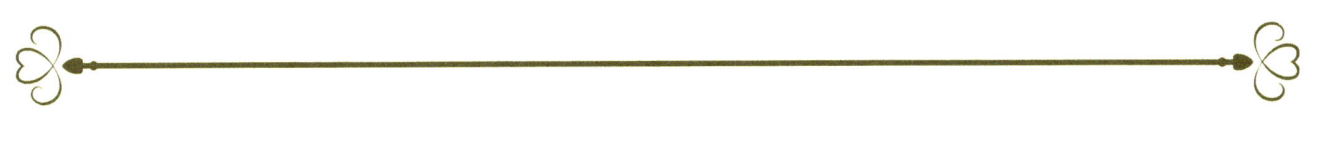

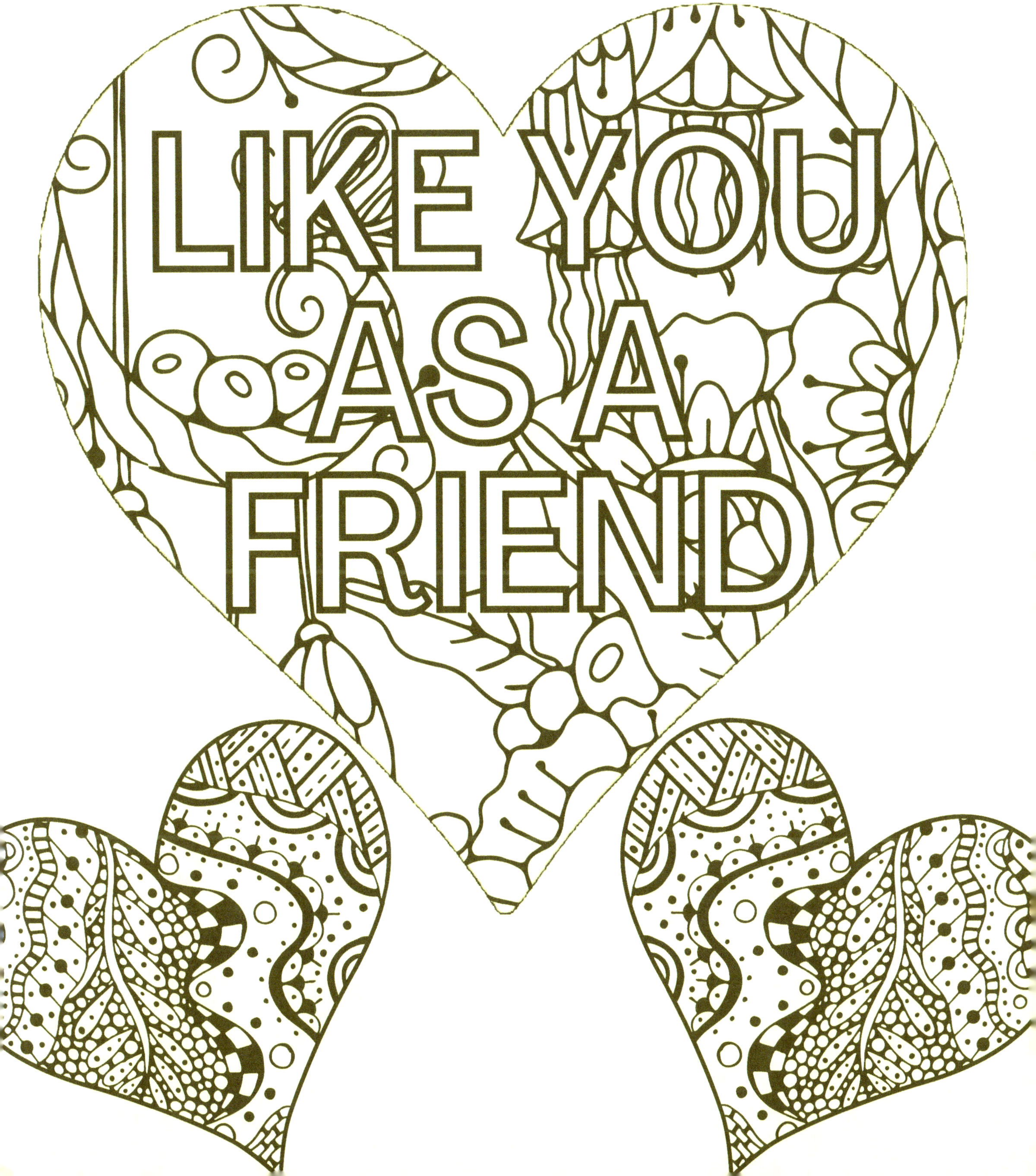

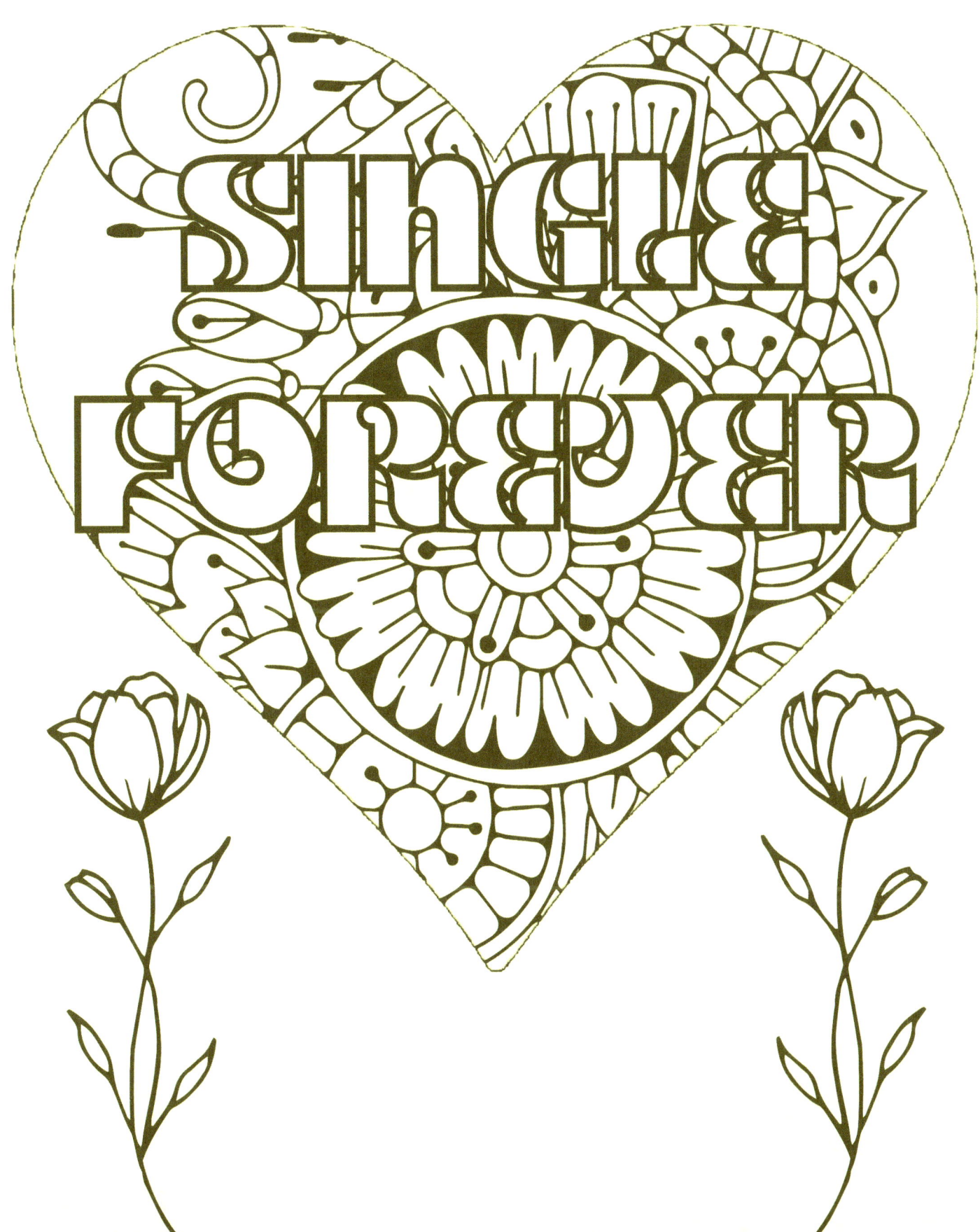

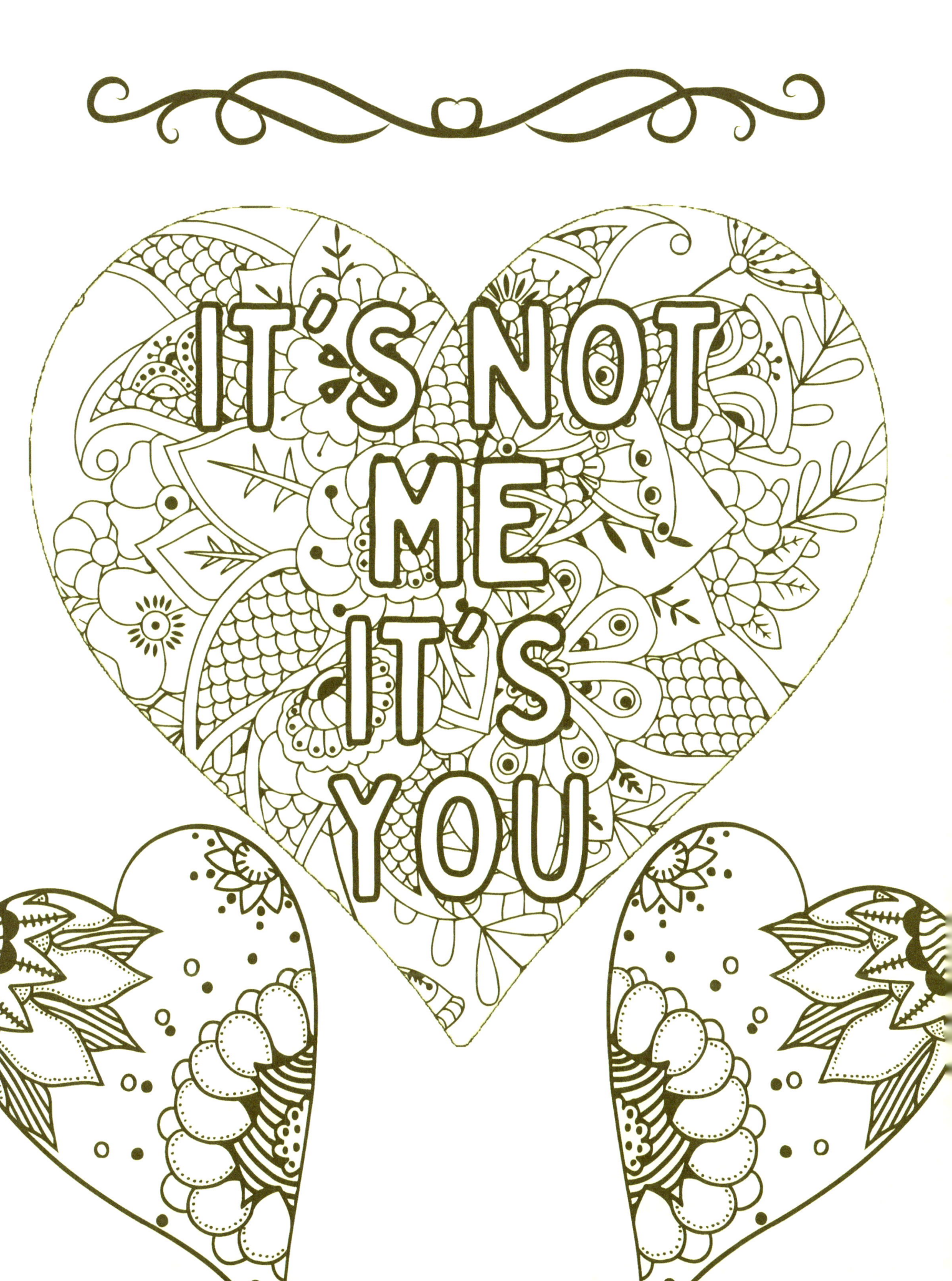

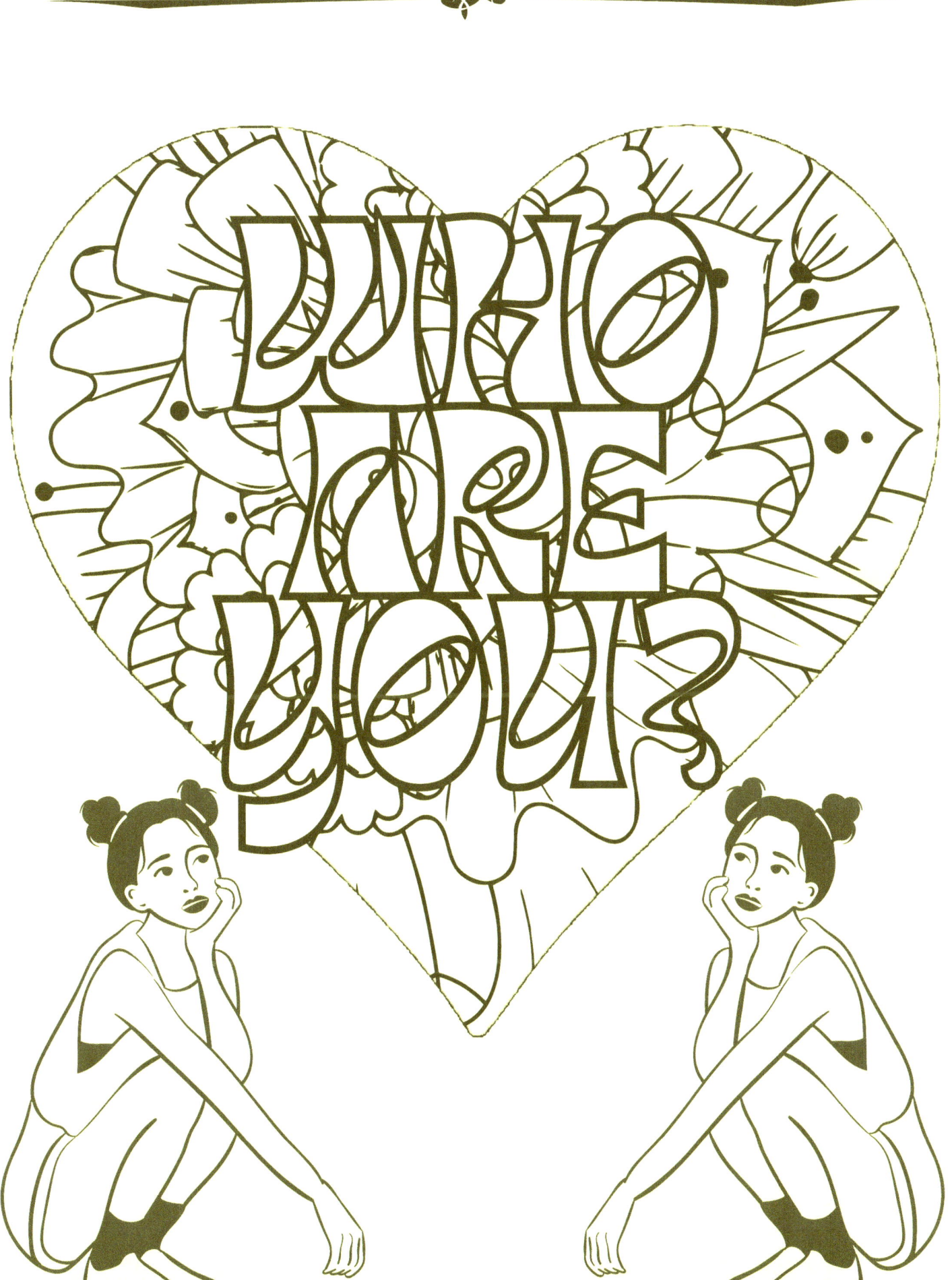

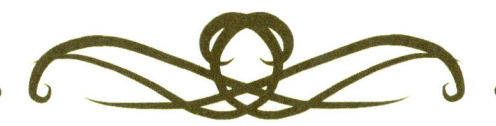

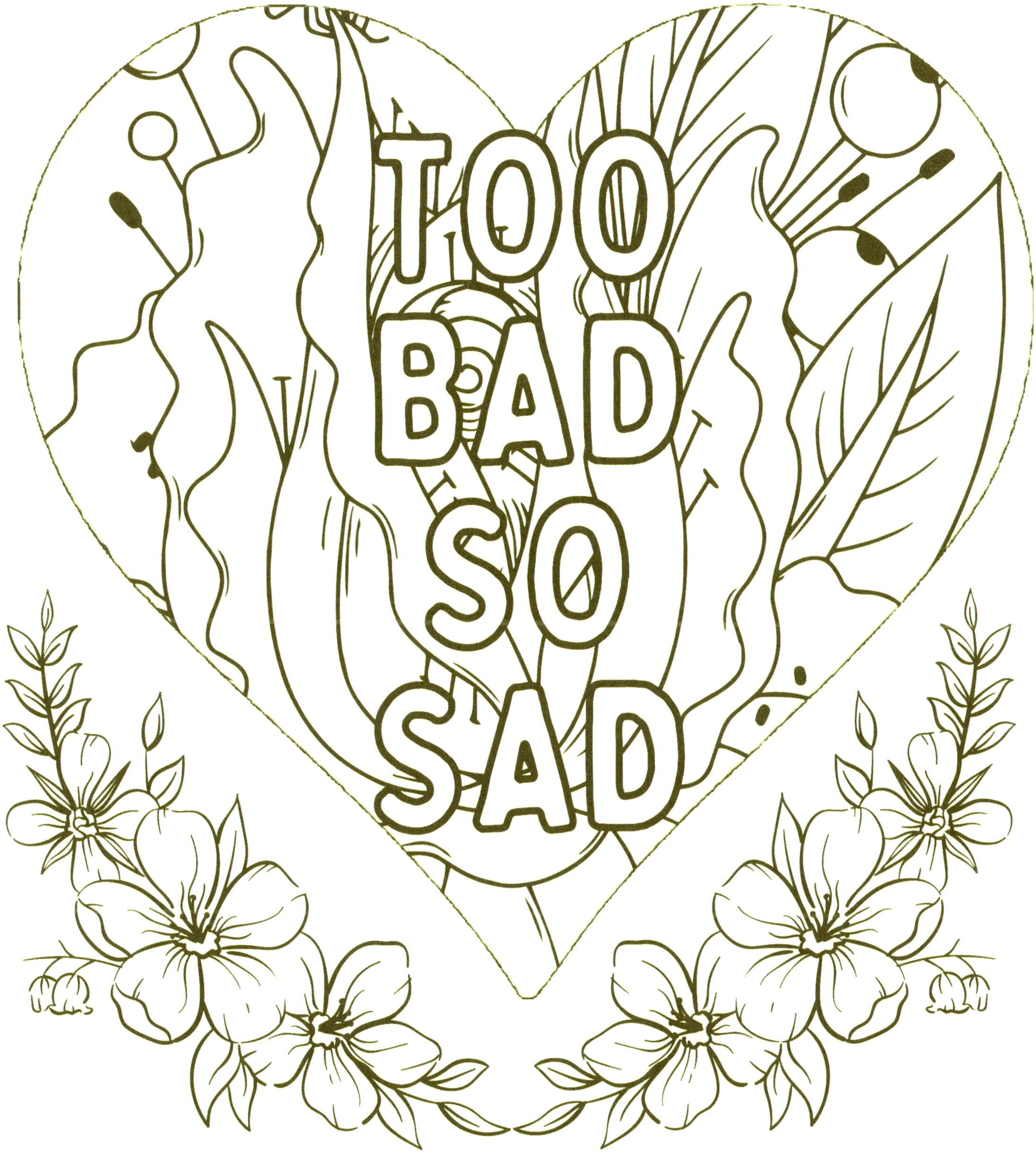

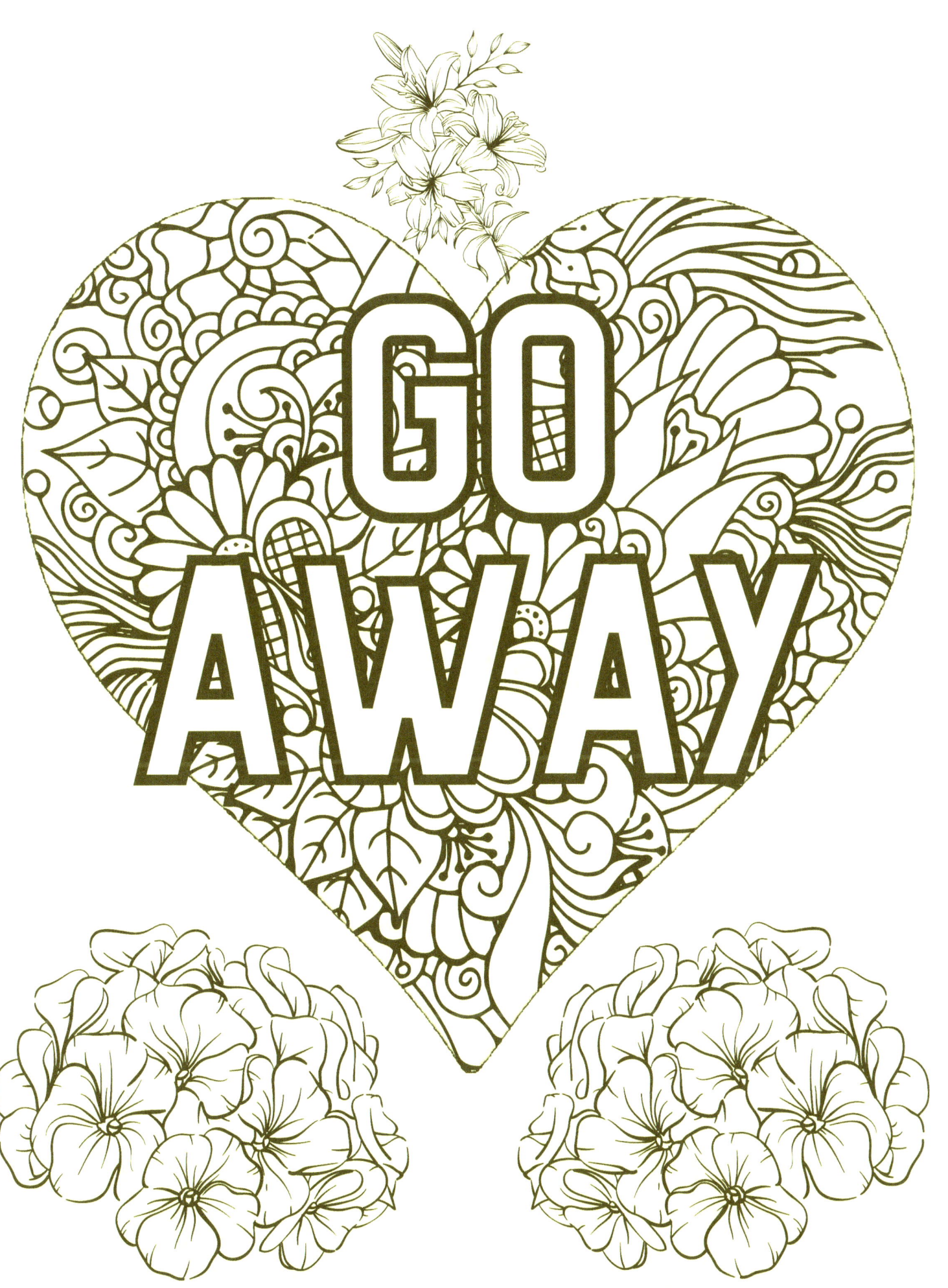

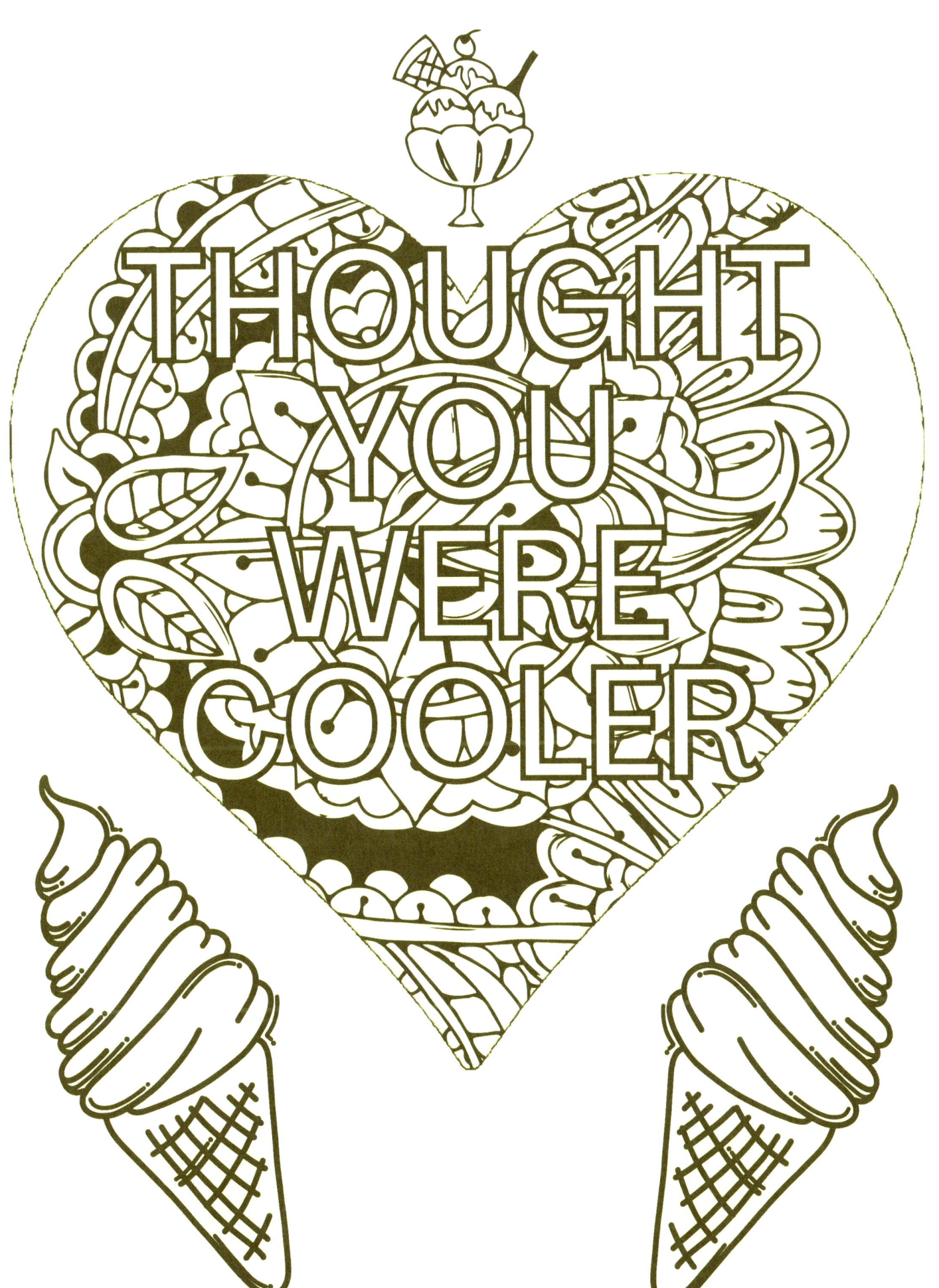

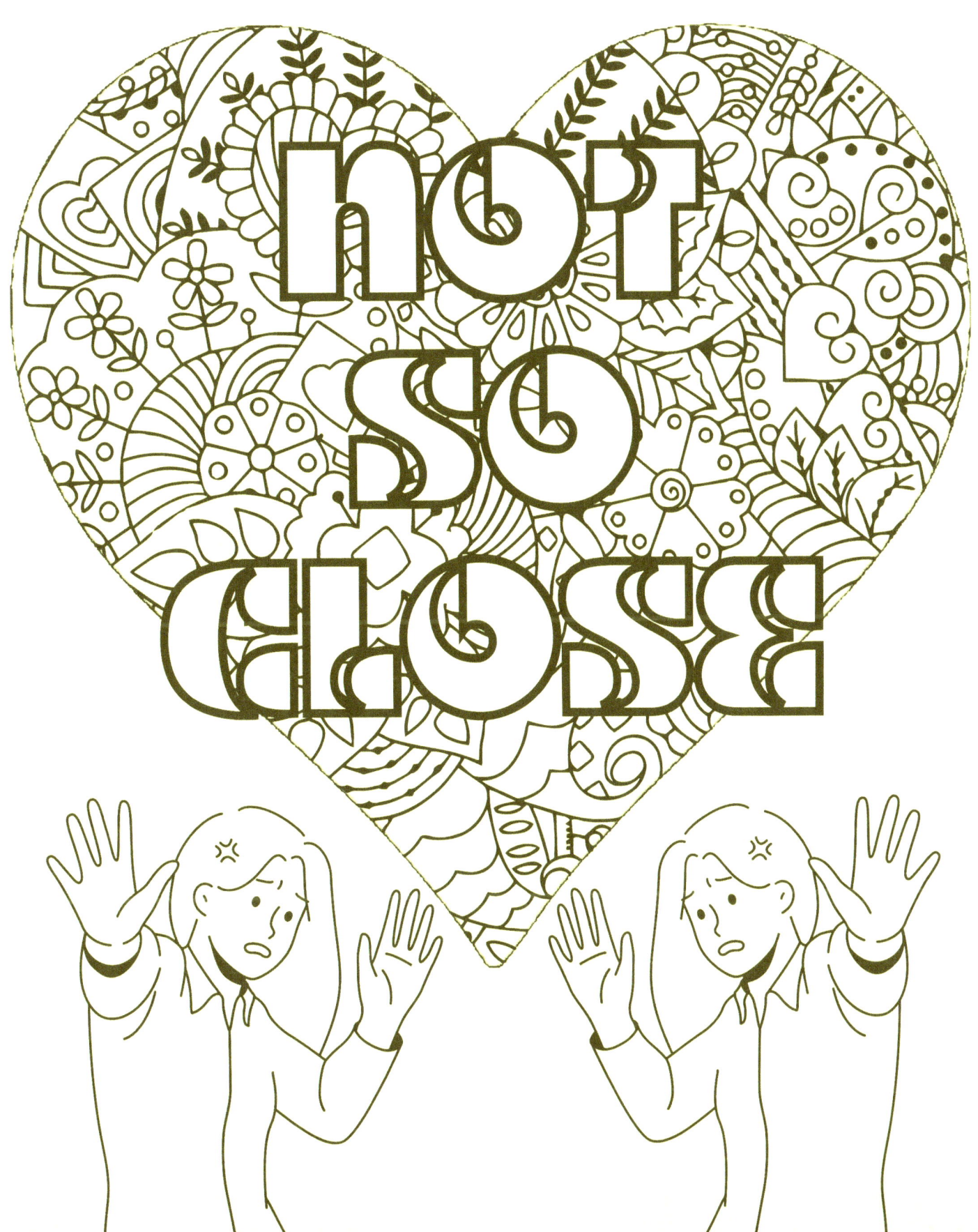

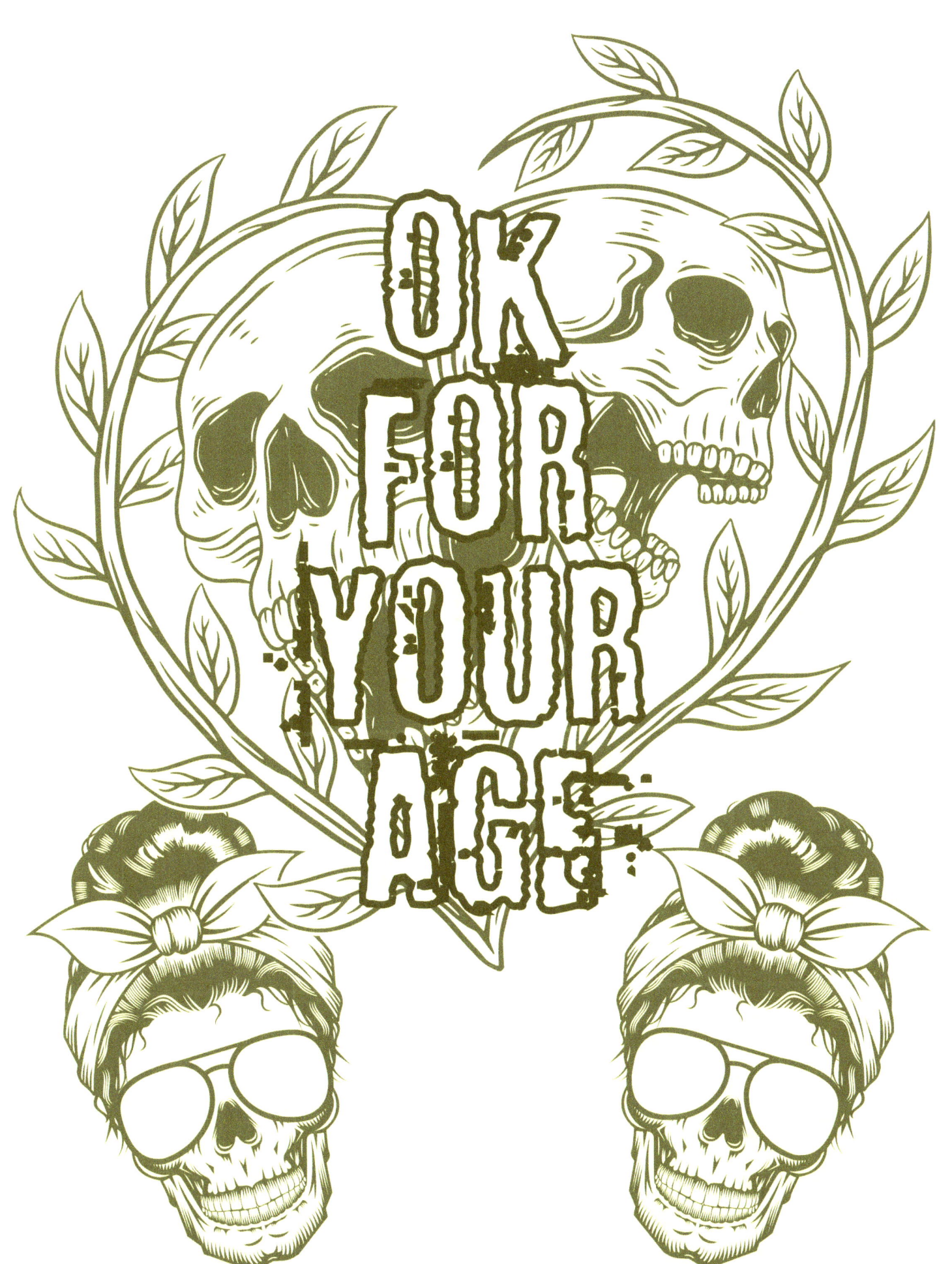

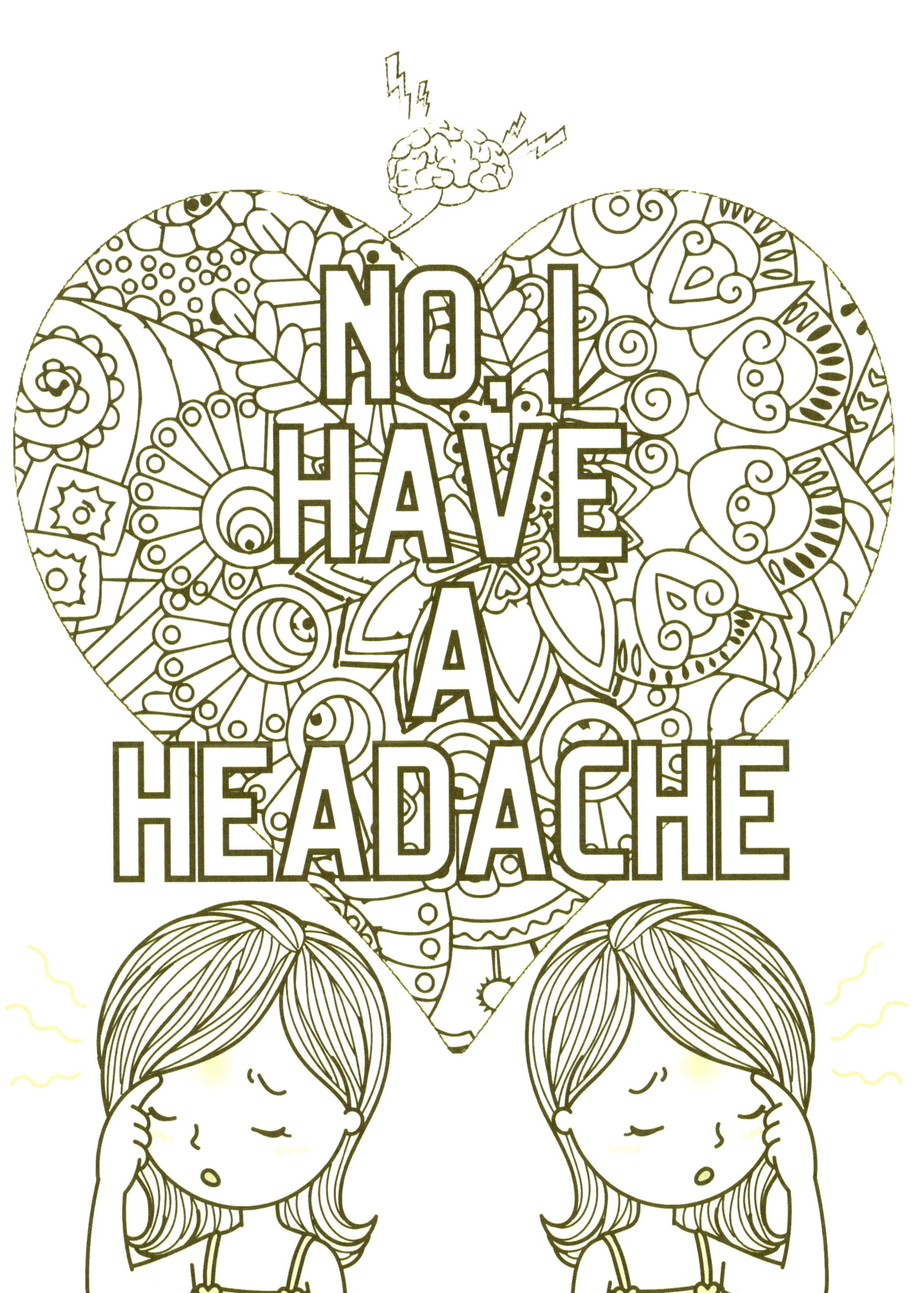

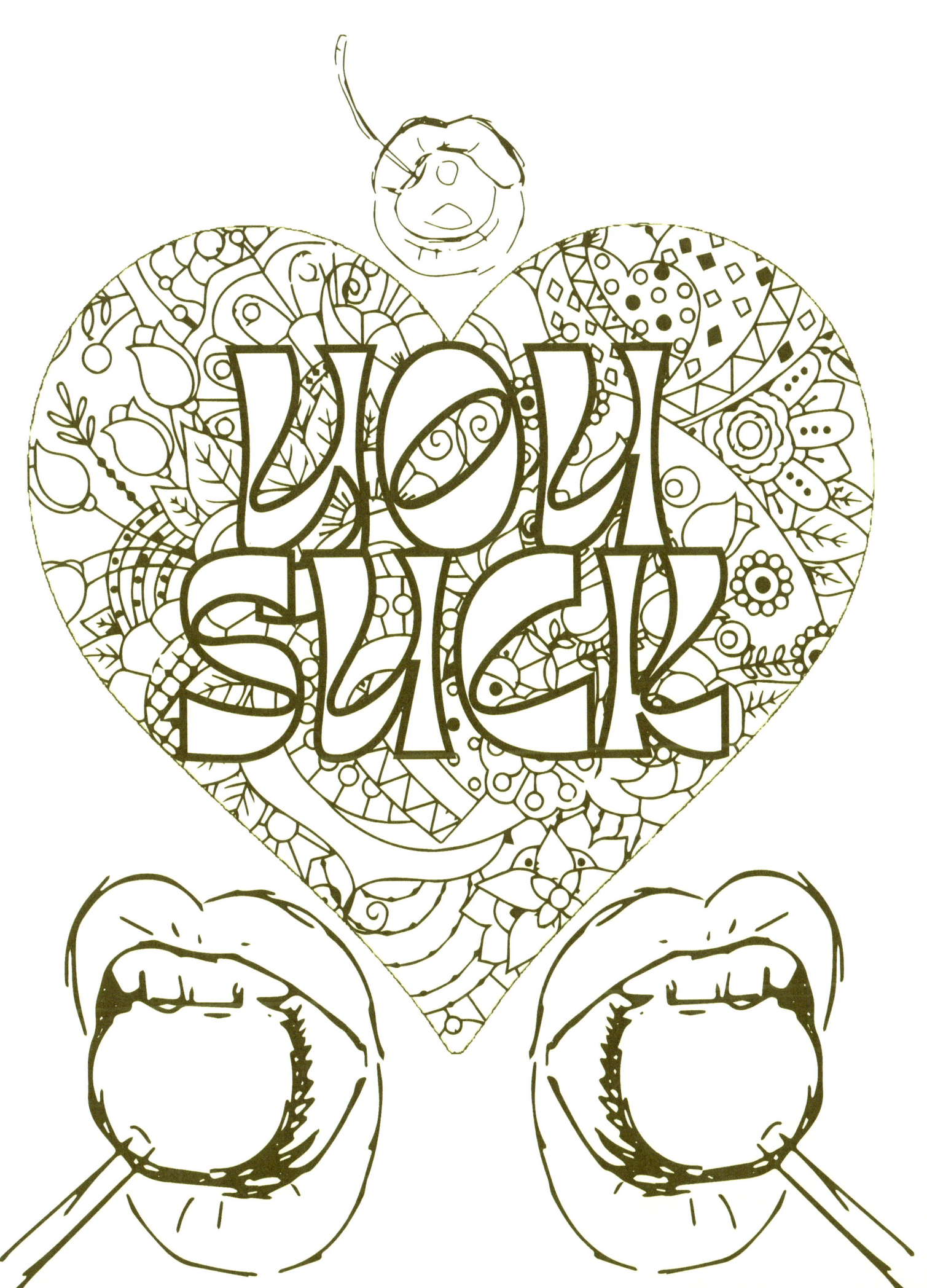

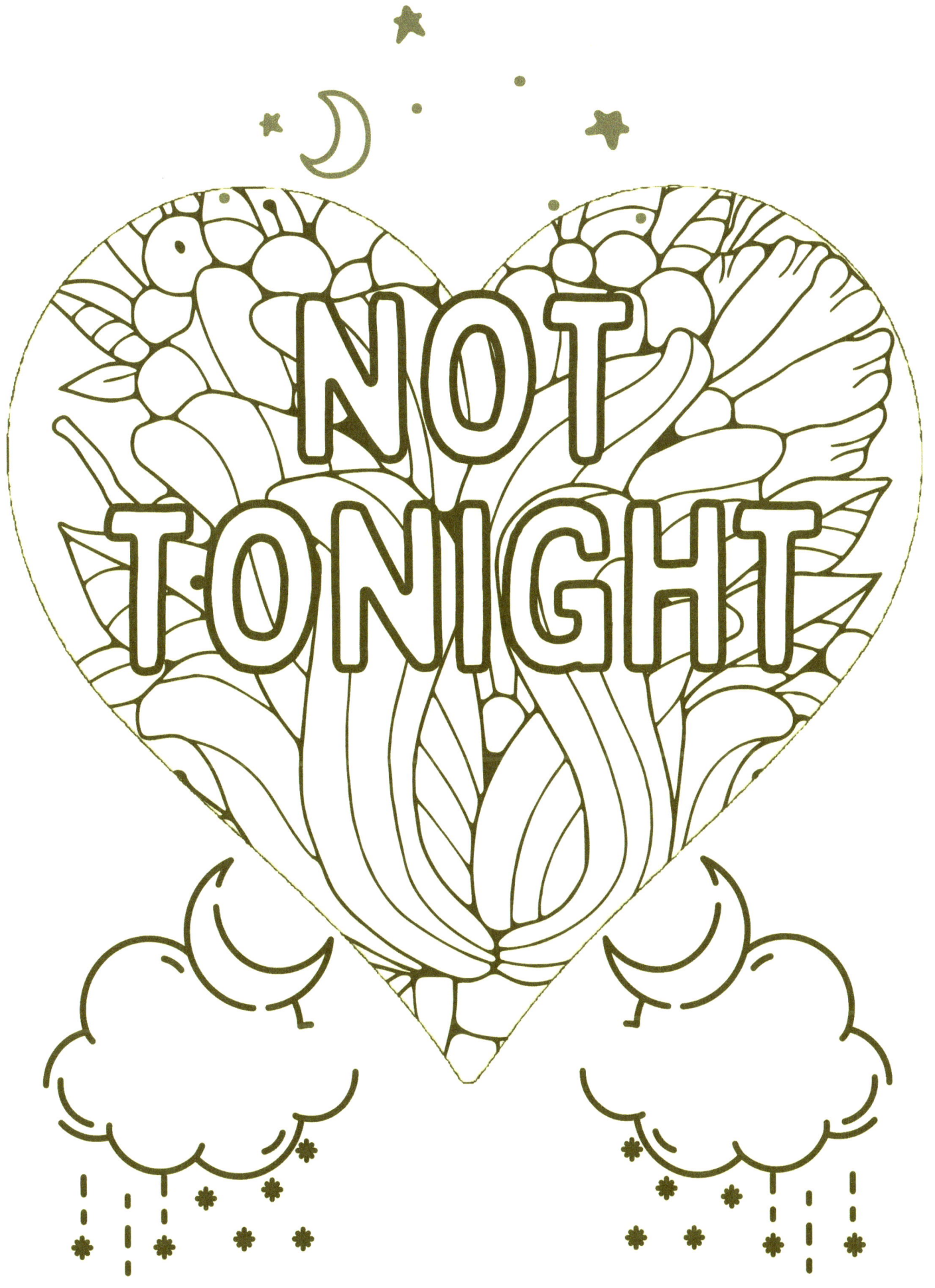

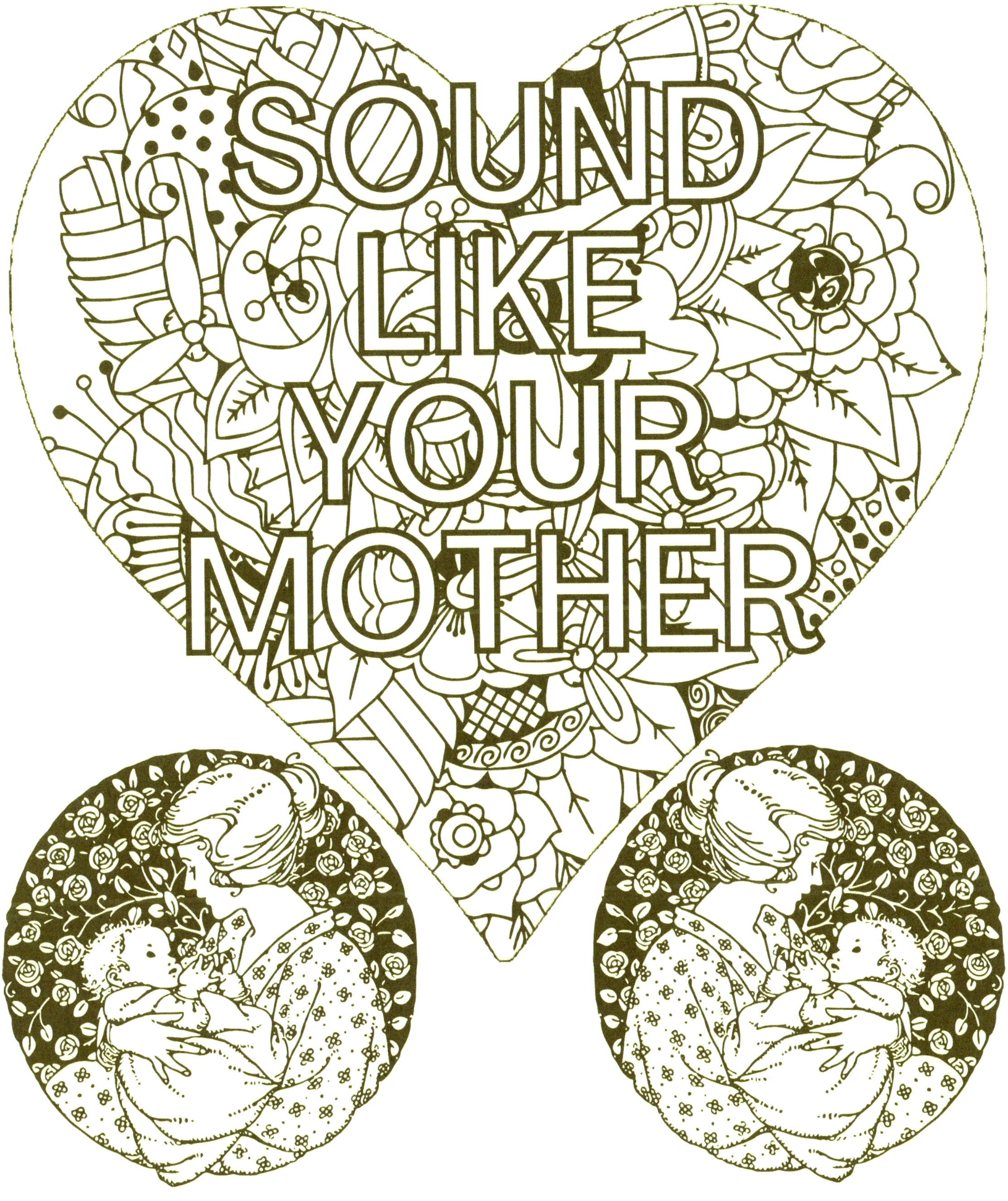

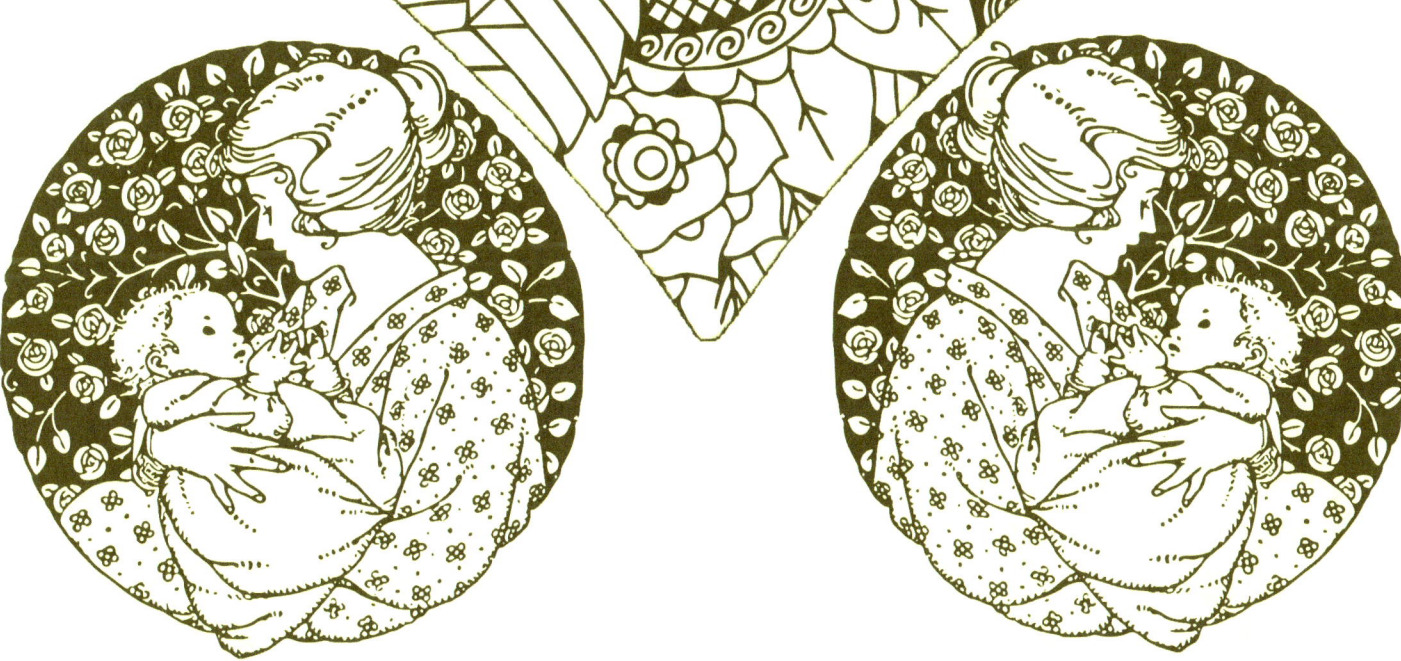

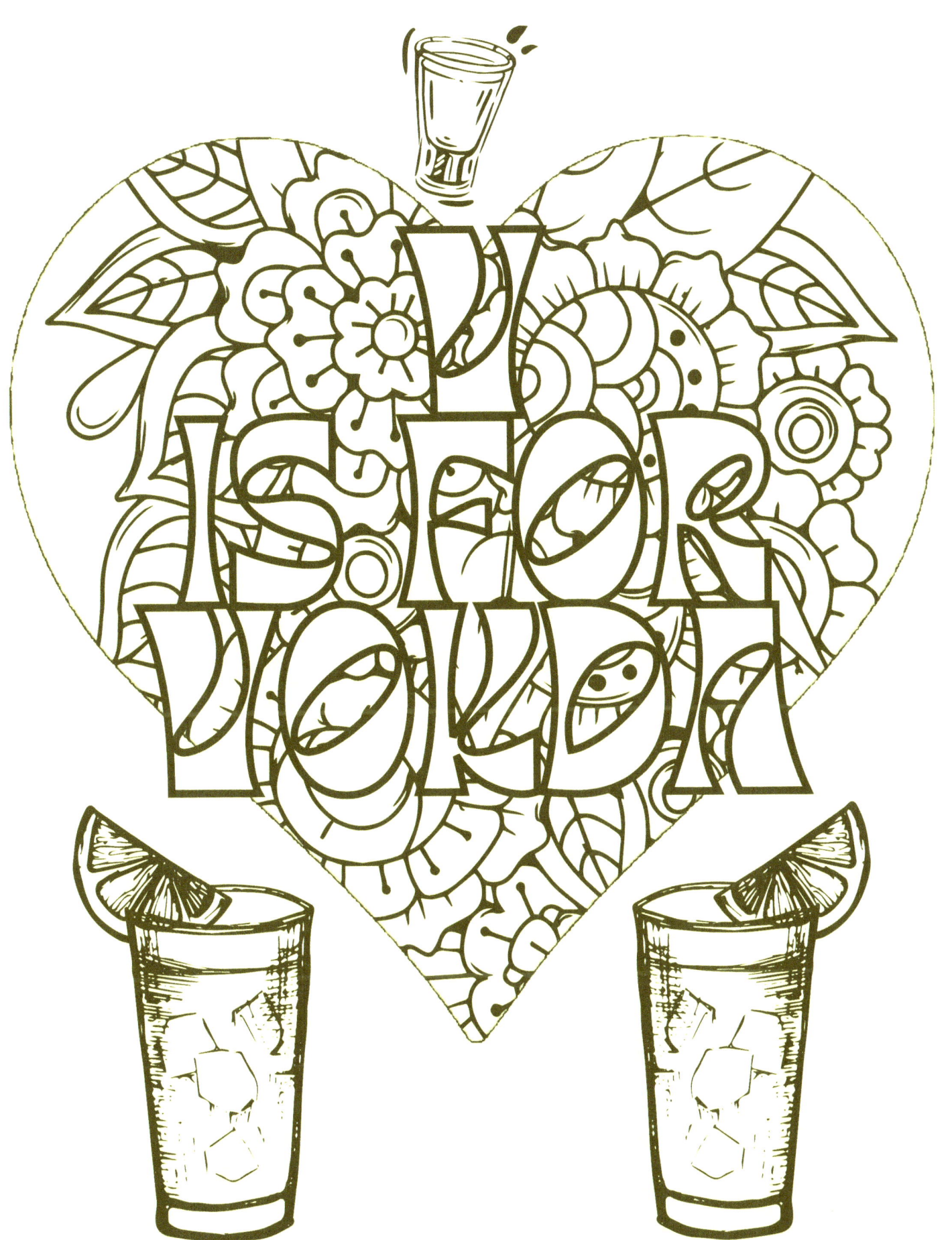

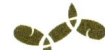

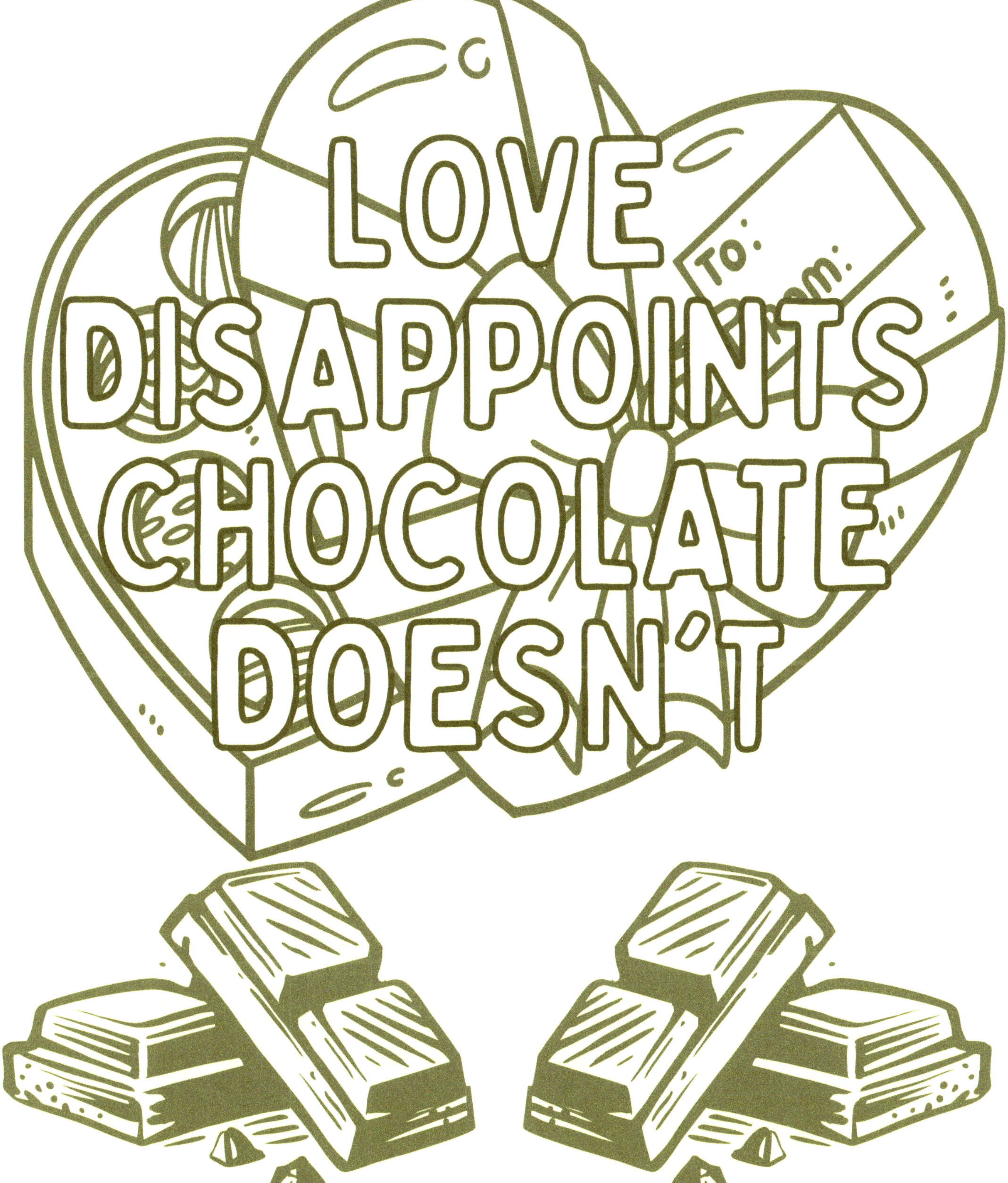

LOVE DISAPPOINTS CHOCOLATE DOESN'T

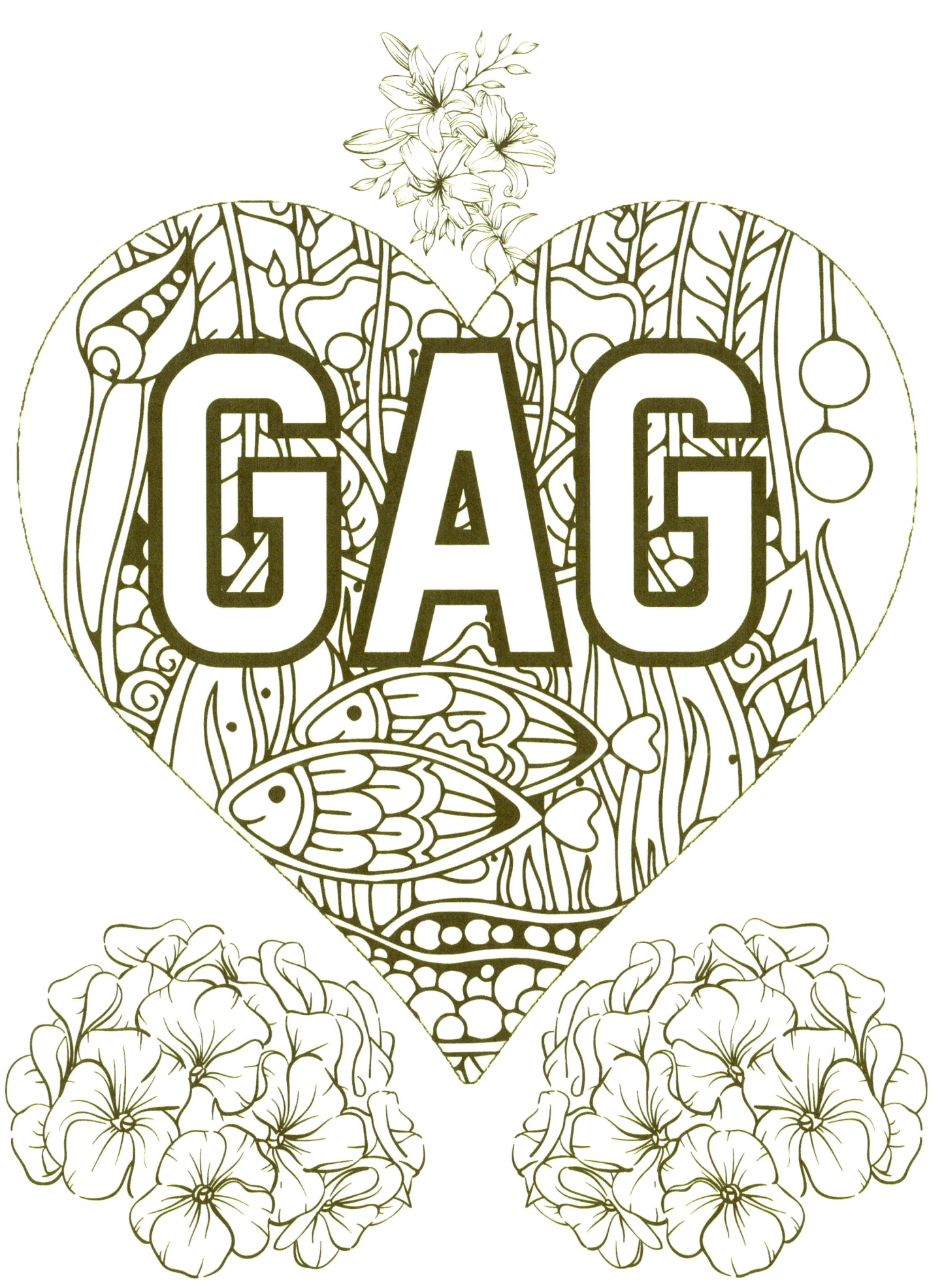

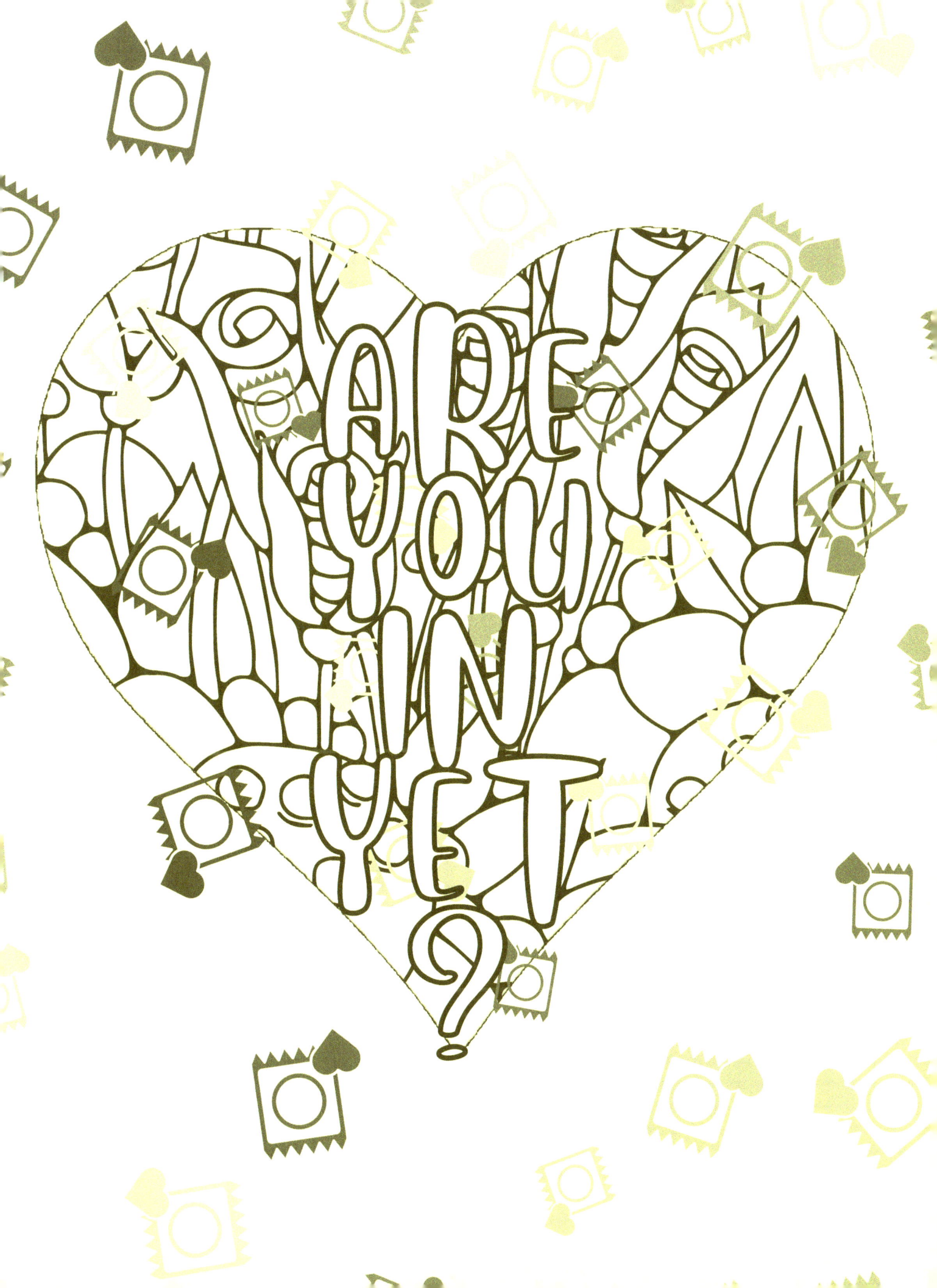

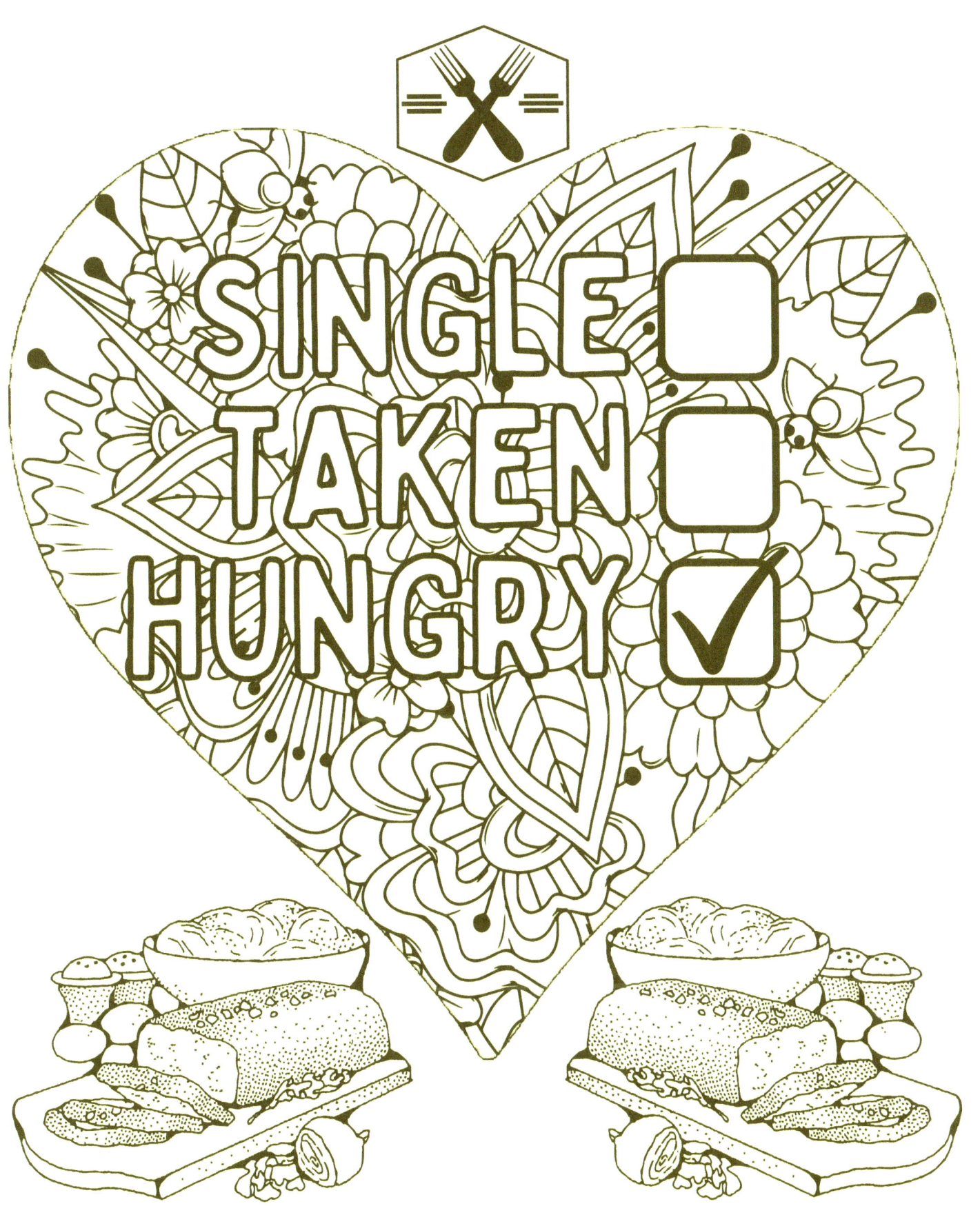

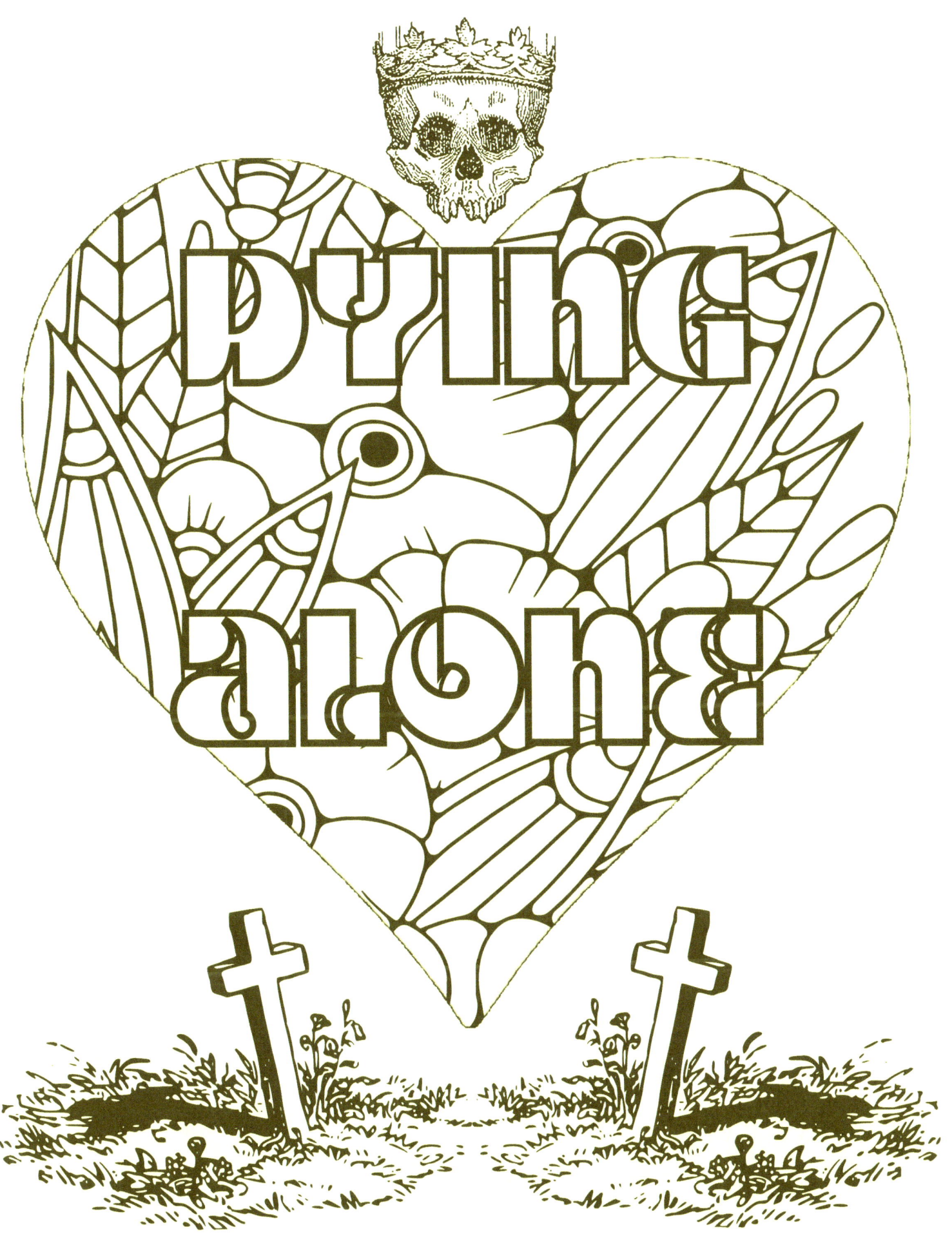

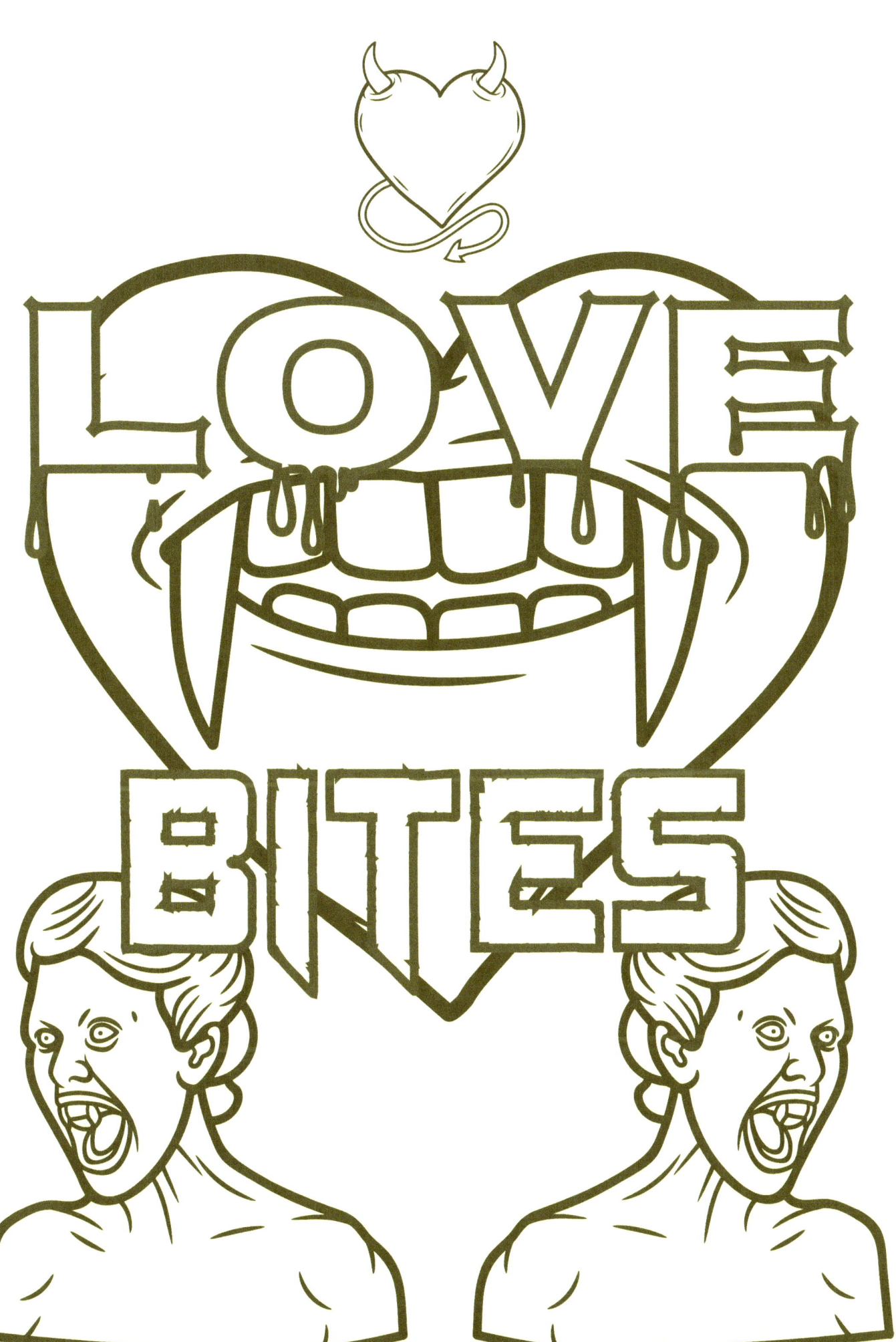

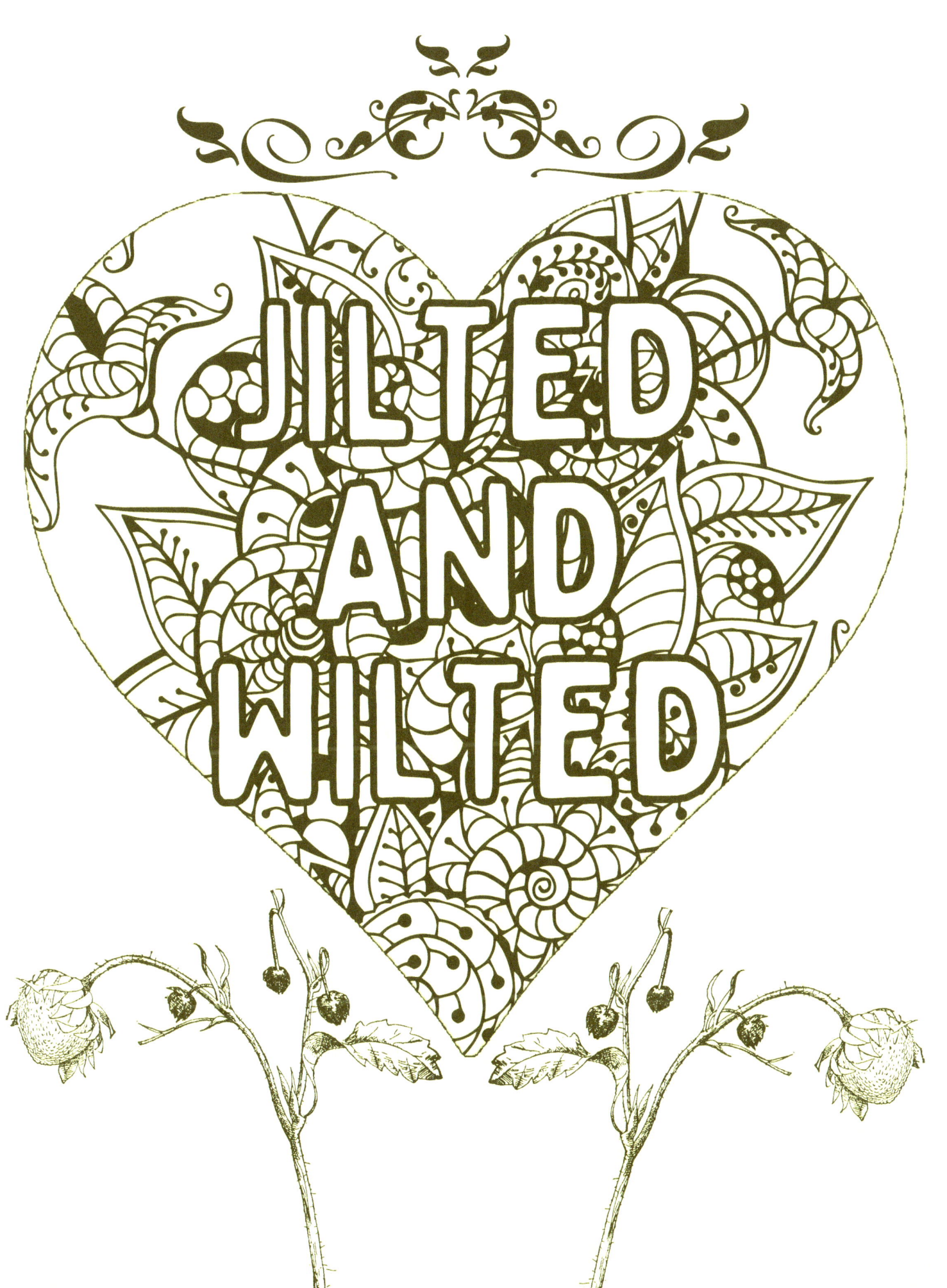

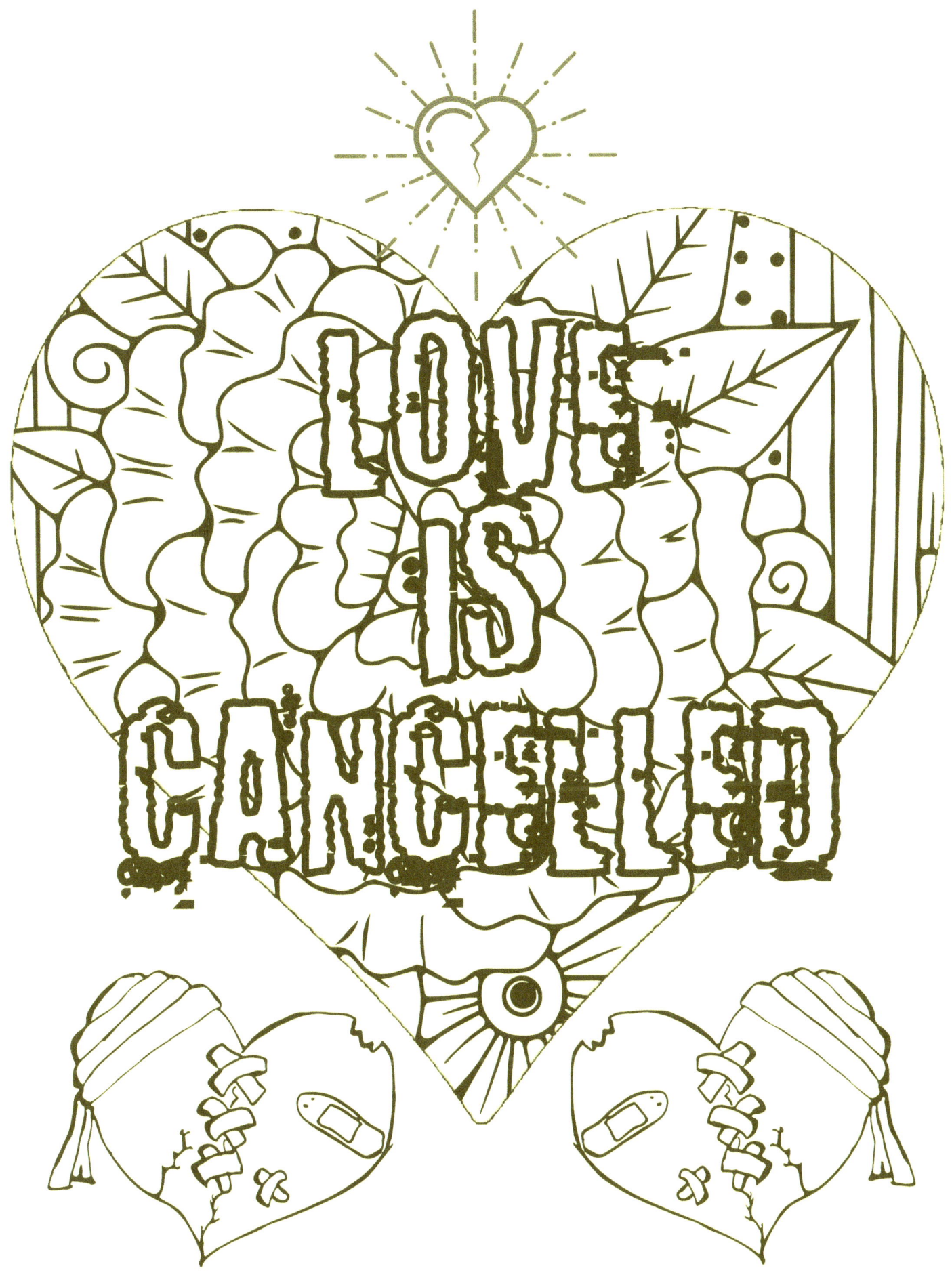

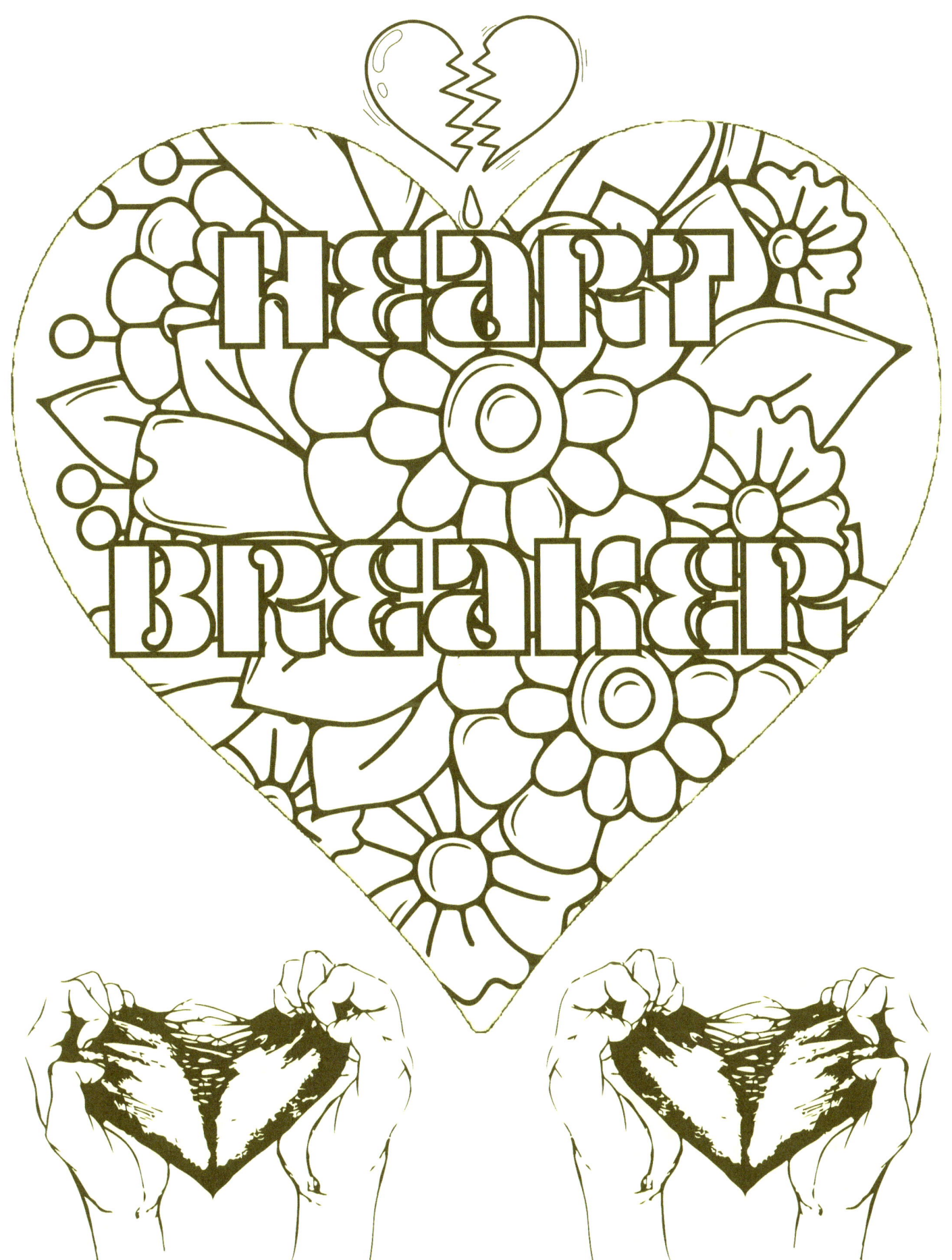

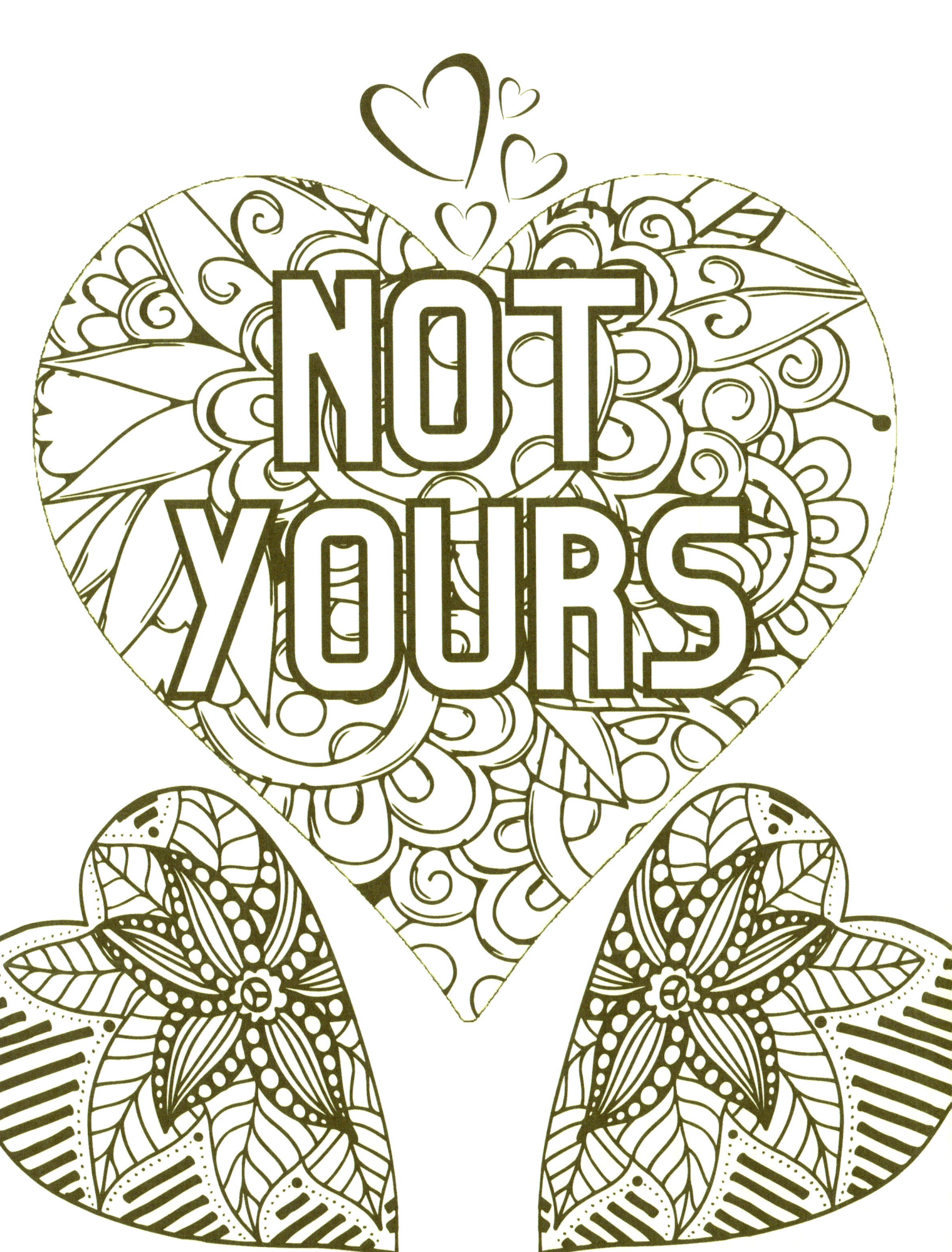

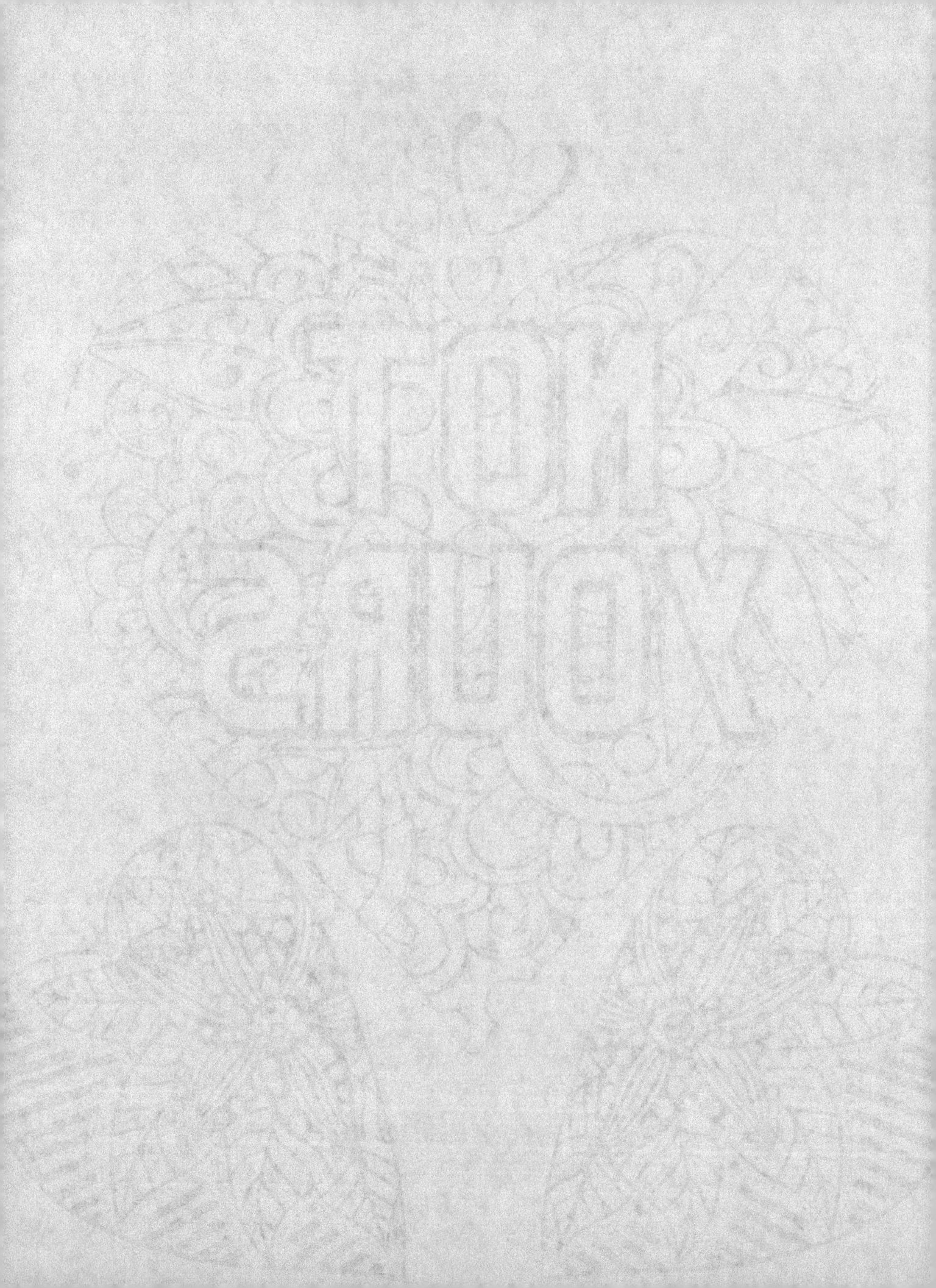

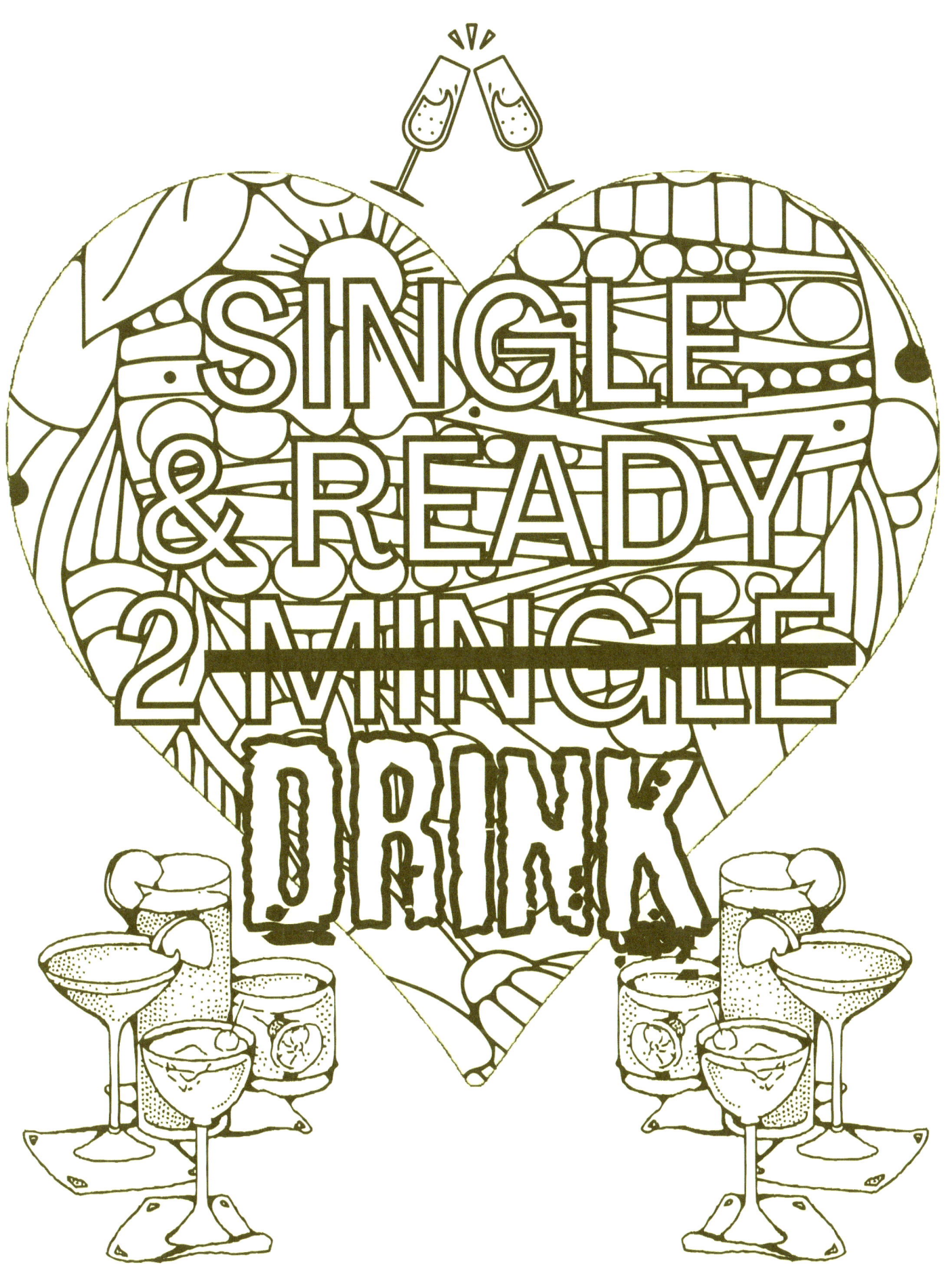

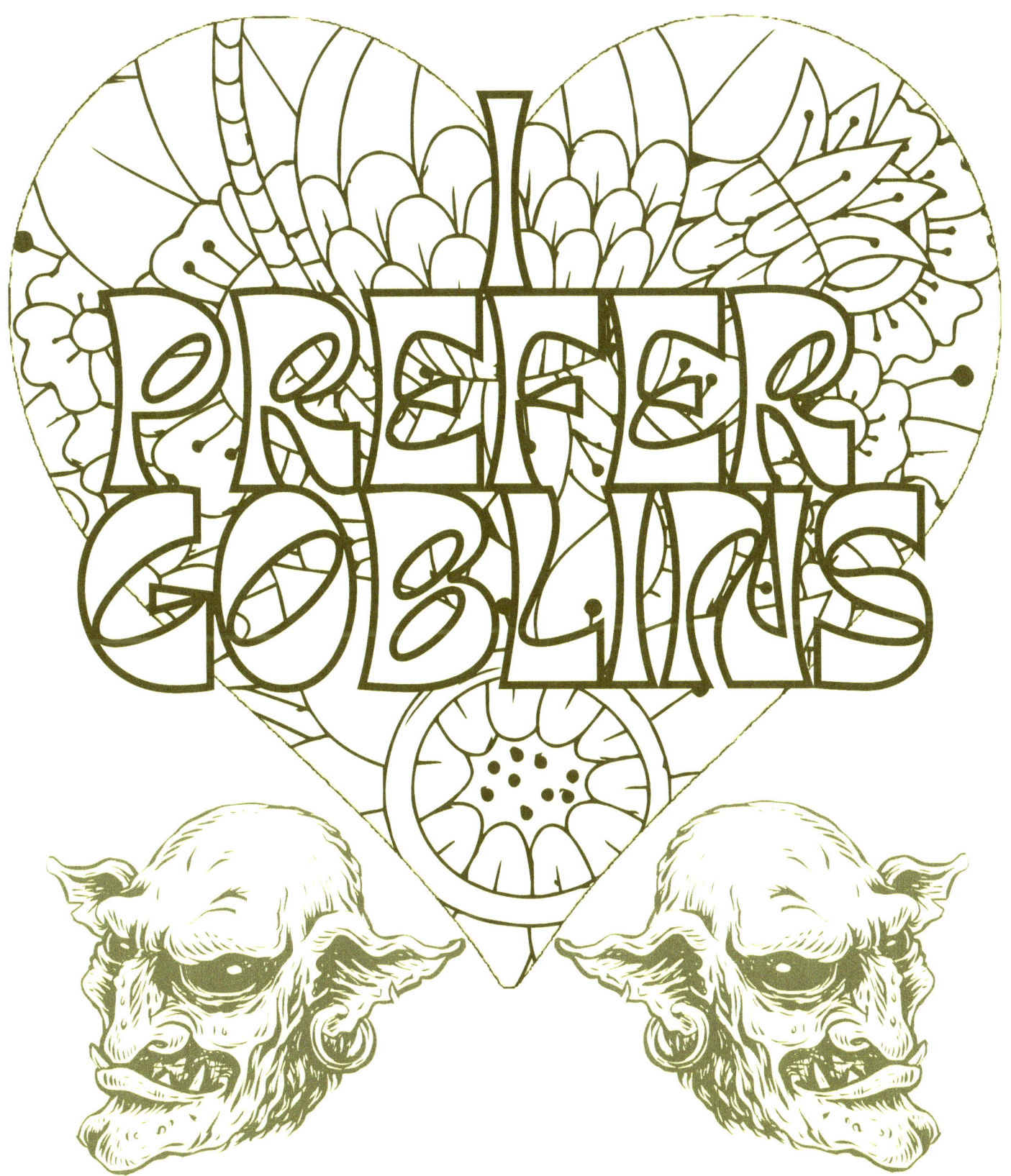

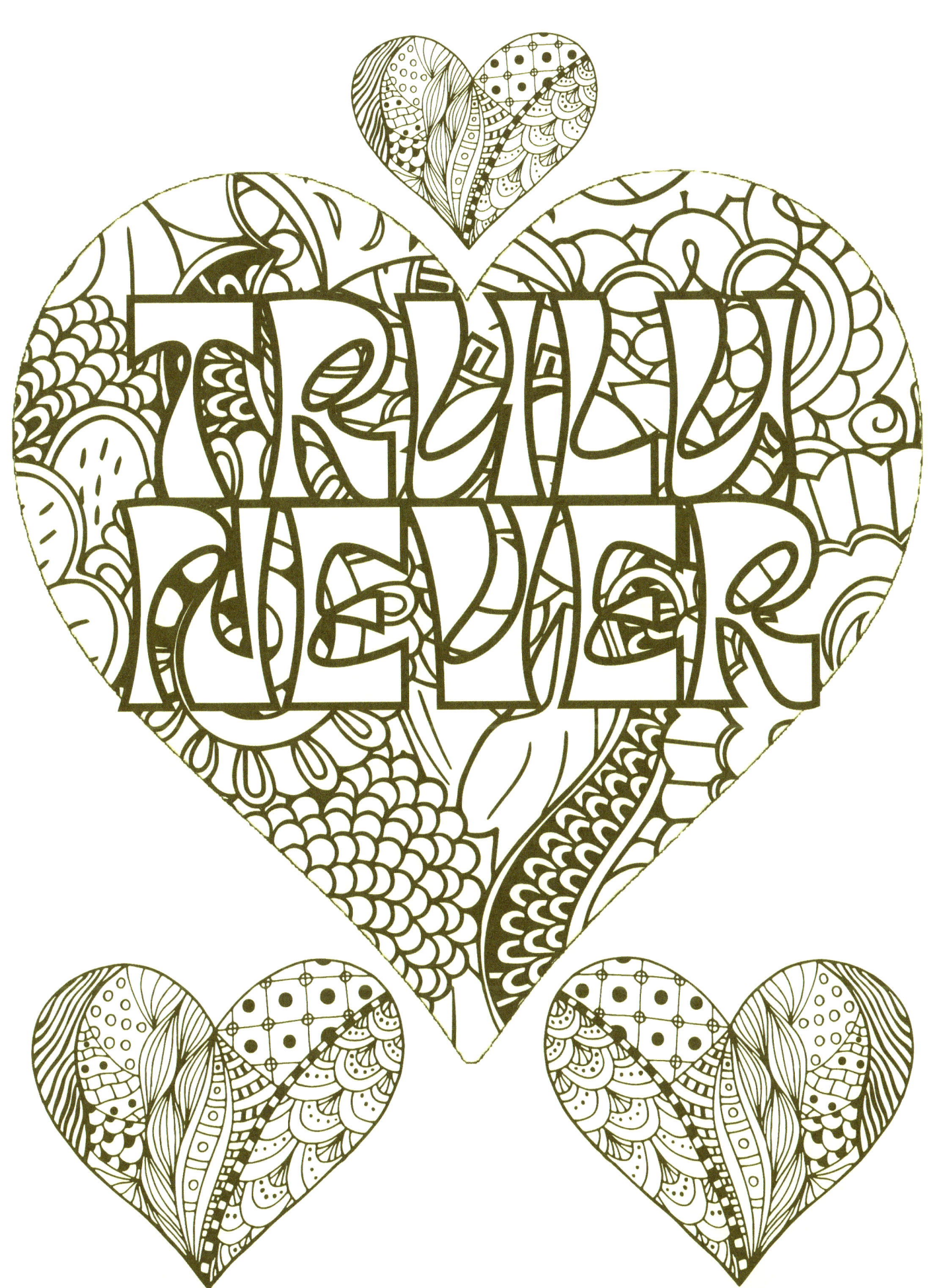

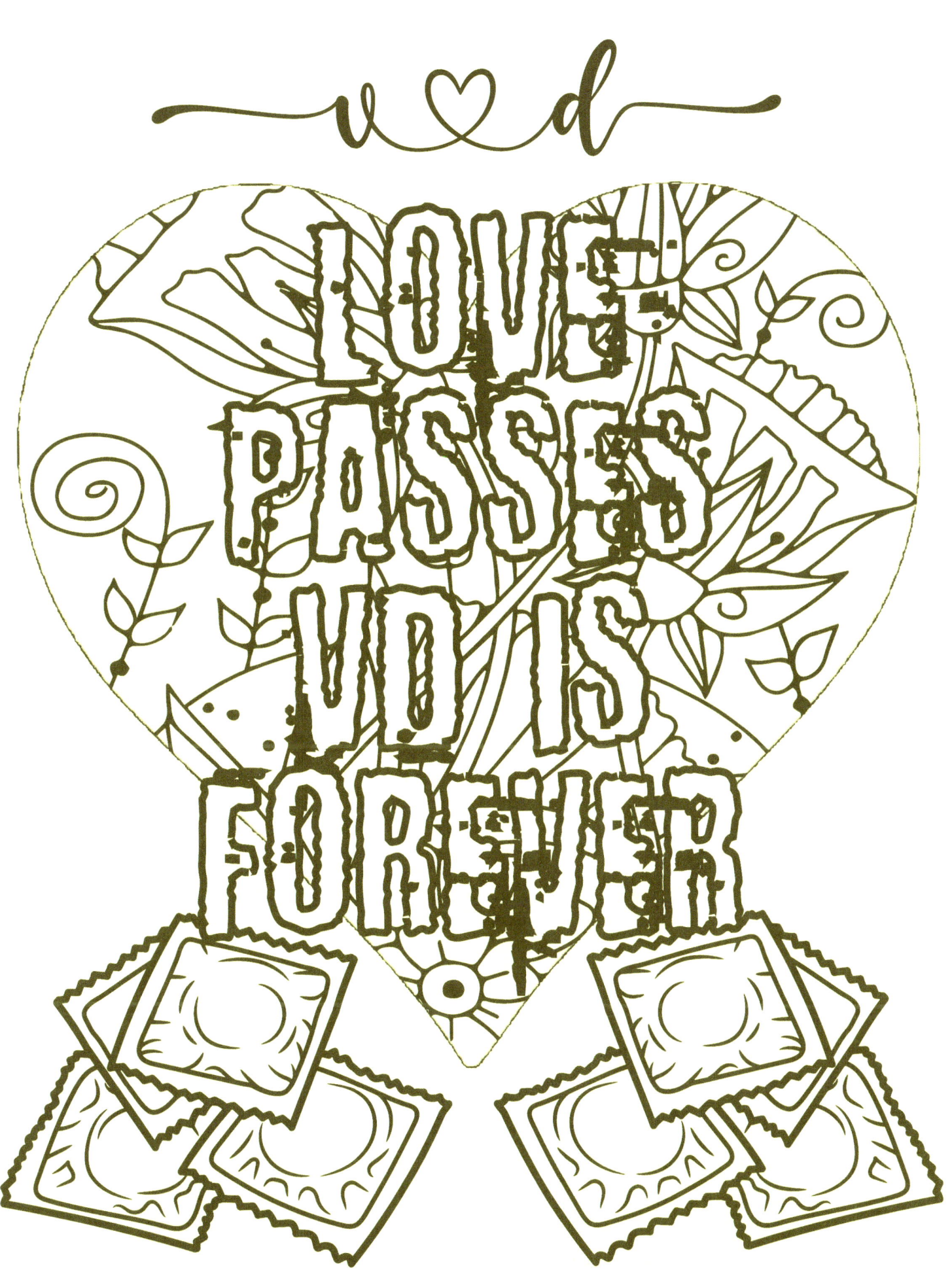

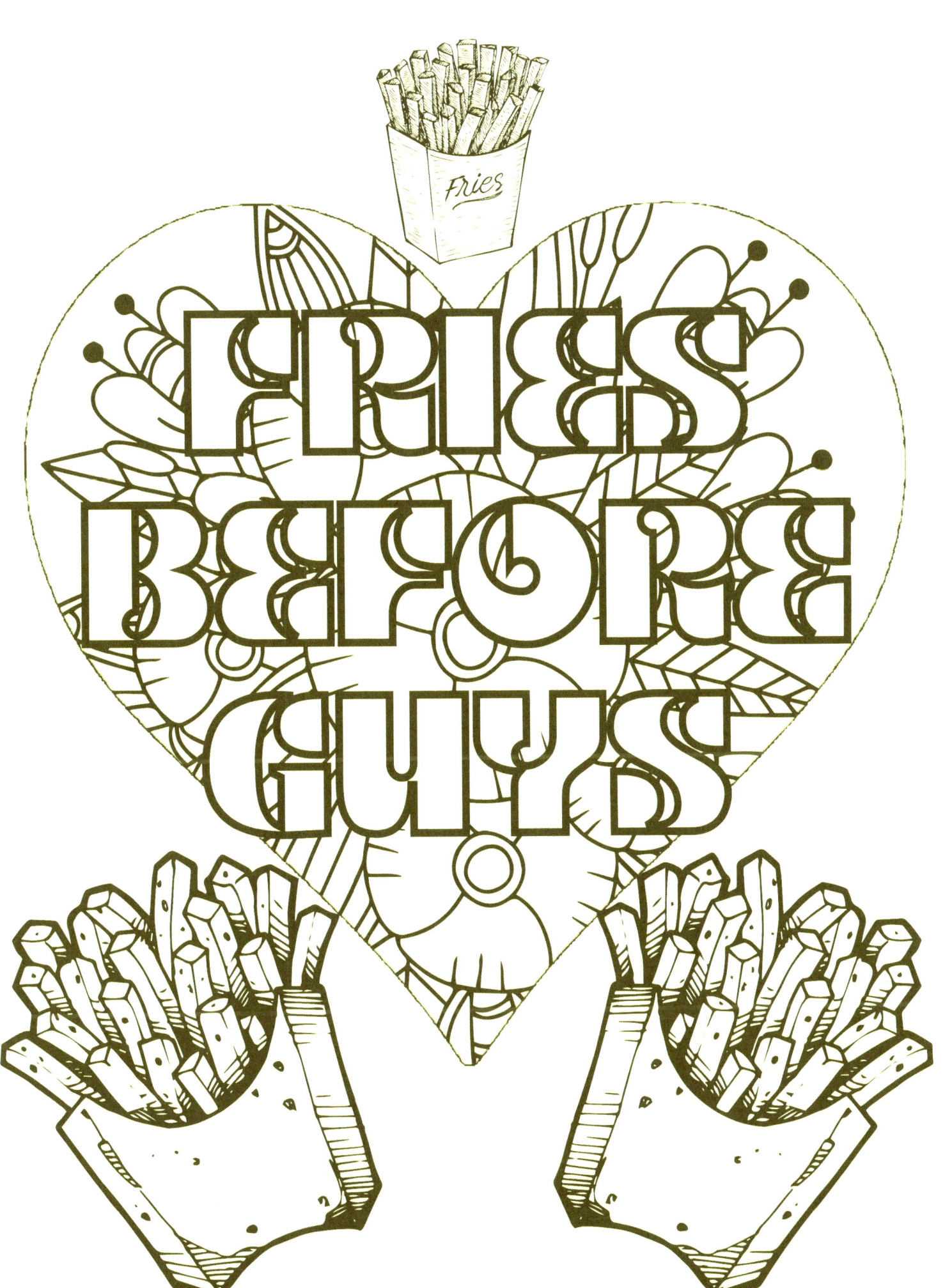

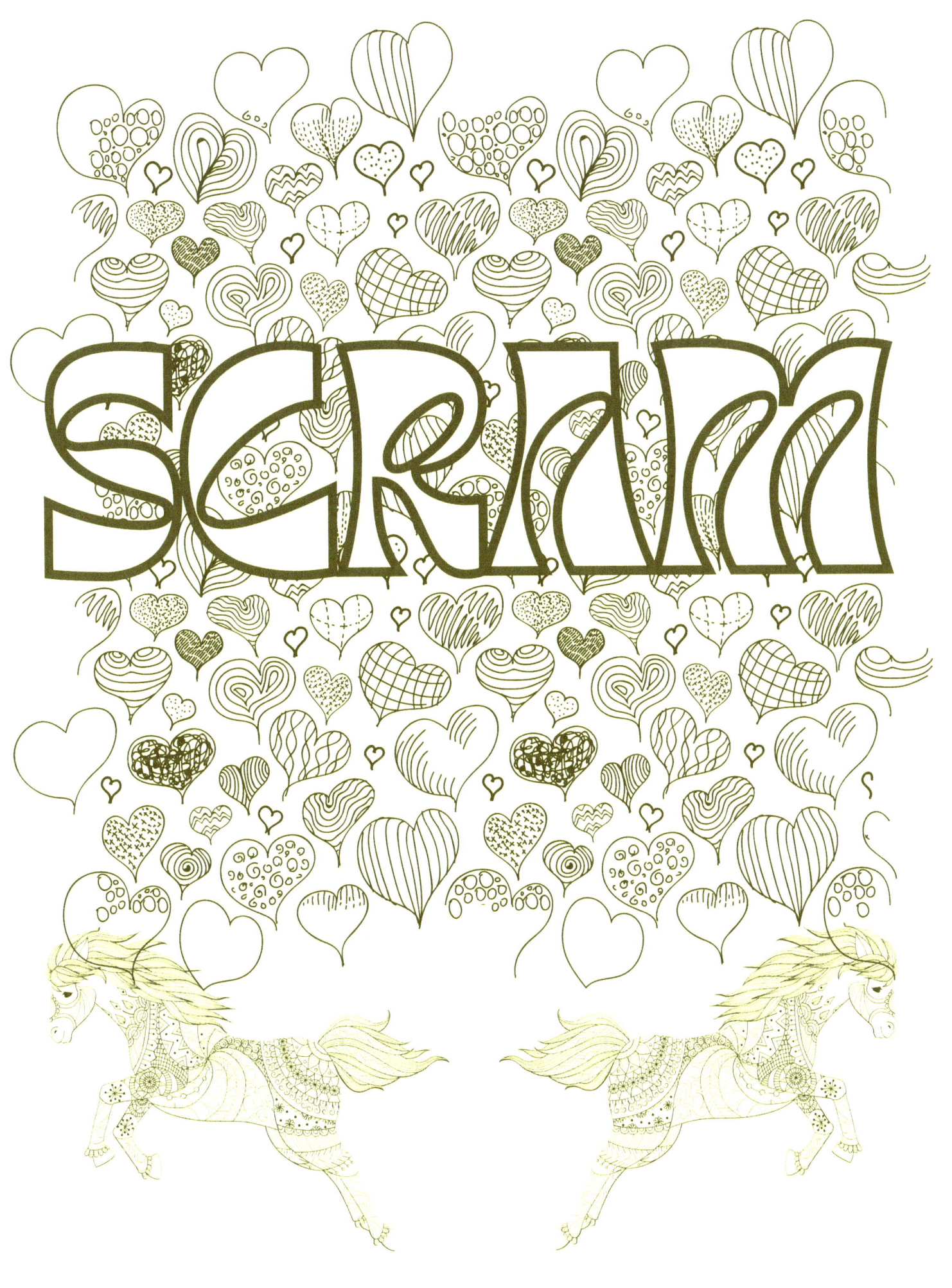

LIKE IT?

PLEASE CONSIDER RATING IT!

www.ingramcontent.com/pod-product-compliance
Lightning Source LLC
Chambersburg PA
CBHW080536220526
45465CB00016B/2337